Imperfect Perfection
By Jonathan Sacker

Imperfect Perfection
By Jonathan Sacker

Dedication

This book is dedicated to Sallie Michele Sacker because she is the most awesome wifey on the planet.

And she is smokin' hot!

Also, because she told me to.

Oh, and this book is also dedicated to everyone with CF that has struggled to survive. No matter what you've gone through and no matter how many times you have felt like giving up, you are not alone. No matter how many trials you've had to crawl through and no matter how much crap you've had to deal with, you are not alone. No matter how many times you've been standing in the shadow of death and felt like it was the end, you are not alone.

And no matter the circumstances or your reactions to those circumstances, you have done well. You have survived. You have battled and run a good race. And you'll continue to do so.

Just make sure to laugh … It is still the best medicine.

Table Of Contents

○ ○ ○ ○ □

Preface-Preamble-Pre-Whatever

○ ○ ○ ○ ☐

This is one of those books that is very hard to place in a single genre. I like to say it is an inspirational dramatic comedy. I'll let you decide though what it eventually becomes for you.

If you are a person obsessed with organization and perfect lines, then this book might frustrate you at different places. There are times where sentences are placed in weird places on the page. This is on purpose. Also, there are purposeful sentence fragments! I know right?

Crazy stuff.

Also, there are people that sometimes just "show up" in the stories. For the sake of clarity, I eventually get around to explaining who they are and how they are related to me. The only one who shows up consistently is my wife, Sallie. And of course, she's the most important anyway!

This is an intimate book, not formal, and is intended to be "absorbed" instead of just read. There are things I say and within those things there are other things being said. There will also be many things I don't say that I expect the reader to be adult enough and mature enough to grasp. It is inside the words, inside the meanings that a reader will find value in this book. Sometimes things are not able to be expressed in words. Feel this book, don't just read it.

   I pray you find strength in this book. The purpose is for those going through the fire, or for those who have gone through the fire, or for those about to go through fire, to find perfection inside of their imperfection.

- Jonathan Sacker

Imperfect Perfection
By Jonathan Sacker

Chapter 1
The Awesome Beginning

○ ○ ○ ○ ▢

"Jonathan Sacker was born in 1980. At his birth, Dr. McCoy and Dr. Spock quickly observed his awesomeness and since then, the world has been a better place. Now, in this current time, the only thing keeping us all from being overrun with calamity and chaos is the understanding that Jonathan Sacker is still awesome..."

- A Famous Dead Guy

I was born in 1980 in the small town of Natchitoches, Louisiana which has a staggering population of around 18,000 people. Obviously from that number you can see it's not the biggest city in the world but it is the most awesome place on the planet since it is where I was born. Unfortunately, as small as the town was, the hospital was equally small and was nowhere ready for my awesomeness. By the way, 1980 just happens to also be the same year that Mt. Saint Helens erupted, which I think was due to the Earth being so excited about my soon arrival that it just couldn't control itself.

In the time of chimpanzees, I was a lizard. I use this term "lizard" because that is exactly what I looked like after about 3 months. I had been cruising along nicely, eating and pooping but at 3 months old, I began showing signs of what the doctors and staff like to term "Failure To Thrive." Instead of being a happy, wide-eyed baby full of excitement and awe, I was a lizard that was all shriveled and malnourished and looked really sick. I spent most of my time coughing, crying, and losing weight so my parents took me to the hospital.

Most of the time babies usually look disgusting and nasty considering the puke and the poop and other junk that they seem to be able to manufacture at an alarming rate but when I was 3 months old, I looked extra "junky." Now, I know all the women reading this book just spazzed out.

"Ah … babies are so cute. You are so mean! I hate this book."

Well, they may be cute but that's only after someone has wiped off all the gross puke and poop and other junk. So, relax, I'm not a baby hater, just a baby puke and poop hater. I love babies … as long as I don't have to kiss them … or smell them … or touch them … and as long as I sit on the other end of the table …

When the doctors saw me, they were a little confused. Since I resembled a lizard, they began treating me immediately for malnutrition. Malnutrition causes babies to look like raisins but I prefer the term "lizard." With hallowed out cheeks and a drawn in mouth, my skin looked dry and scaly like crumpled leather. Most of the effects of my malnutrition were temporary but I still have scars around my mouth that look like thin grooves about five centimeters in length that can be found on the left and right edges of my lips. These scars were from my lips being drawn in extremely tight with little flexibility. When I was a teen I used to tell girls that I got in a fight with a bear in the woods and the thin grooves were where the bear clawed at my face. I know, you are thinking it so I'll just say it.

That is so awesome.

I have a scar from a deep tissue sample they took out of my right thigh. This was done to help determine what kind of problem they were dealing with and how to go about with treatment but in reality the doctors were freaked and completely out of their element. They really never had any definitive results to help in their quest to understand what was making me so sick and causing me to not thrive. After coming up with basically nothing, the doctors began looking into environmental factors that might have caused my malnutrition and illness. They began interrogating my parents and even threw around the idea that they had withheld foods and nourishment causing me to fail to stay healthy.

I'm sure this was traumatic for my parents. For three months they had done everything they could to get me to eat and grow. They had prayed and sought God every night for me to breathe well and stop coughing but nothing they did seemed to work. Nothing they did seemed to help. And now, after bringing their baby to a place that was supposed to have answers, they were not only getting nothing helpful but were now prime suspects in a "Failure To Thrive" case.

The doctors of this small hospital were simply unprepared for this type of problem. Without the correct education and training, they were unable to save this baby because they had never encountered anything that even remotely resembled this type of sickness. To them, all they saw was a shriveled lizard baby that was reacting negatively to everything and they were helpless.

Since doctors don't usually stand around and let lizards die, more proverbial tests were run and more blood was examined under microscopes by those brainy people who wear glasses but still look trendy. The problem proved to be too overwhelming for the small hospital and so the know-it-all doctors called in a know-it-all specialist that just by chance happened to be there. Strange how they are always coincidentally there at the specific time they are needed.

This specialist was very special. She had been specializing for a long time and when she saw the baby boy that looked more like a lizard-boy, she knew immediately that something weird was going on. This baby boy, upon her special decree, was awesome. Not just your average, run-of-the-mill awesome, but much more supernaturally awesome than anyone else had ever been. For this reason, and this reason alone, Bettina Hillman, one of the foremost pediatric specialists in the universe, who just happened to be in Natchitoches, Louisiana, diagnosed this awesome baby boy with Cystic Fibrosis...

...and the world was forever changed.

   With one look, she was able to diagnose Cystic Fibrosis. They ran a sweat test which is the standard test used to determine Cystic Fibrosis by measuring the amount of chloride that is excreted in a person's sweat. After passing the test and confirming that I was absolutely awesome, my parent's life then went into overdrive. The specialists and doctors began infusing the lizard...err, baby boy, sorry, brain lapse...with medicines that cleared up the malnourishment and weirdness. These medicines also helped counter the infection that had caused my coughing and after a few days and a lot of stress and painful, tear streaked nights for the parents, the baby boy named Jonathan Sacker was finally able to go back home.

Chapter 1.5
A Glimpse Of The Extraordinary

○ ○ ○ ○ ▢

This was nearly thirty two years ago to this year. I have sometimes tried to imagine what took place but of course as you can see my imagination is large and a little out of control. It's hard for me to imagine a mother, excited to give birth to her first baby, seeing that beautiful baby finally emerge but so sick and so very weak. It's hard for me to connect to a mother's heart that feels like it is going to break to pieces at the sight of a baby that is not as perfect as she's been imagining through the past nine months.

She's been so excited, so scared, so anxious, and praying constantly that she'd be a good mother. She's been quietly planning and quietly conducting herself so carefully for the day when her baby would come to live with her. Carrying a gift from God that is above and beyond anything she's ever been given and reverencing the amazing miracle that makes it able for a human being to live inside a mother, she cares and pampers her body so that this perfect child can come and live in her world. But, this mother did not get to experience this birth in nearly any way she had ever imagined.

She sees her perfection in an imperfect and different way. She sees her dreams and aspirations for this child and her plans and desires for his life begin to take different forms.

Immediately she is assaulted by the changes that she'll have to make in her life, not just temporarily, but forever. Her life is not her own. In this, she is connected to all mothers, for the birth of a child makes the parent's life absolutely change to the form of servant. But that is the only real similarity between herself and the woman next door in the delivery room who just gave birth to perfection.

Perfection is born with imperfection. Perfection nearly dies there in the hospital, where perfection was supposed to be born without imperfection. She watches helplessly as her perfection struggles to breathe, struggles to gain weight, and struggles to just survive. Then, at the lowest points, she is even accused of being an imperfect mother. She questions a perfect God, questions fate, questions it all and walks through the valley of imperfection and can barely see due to all the shadows of death that reach towards her.

They threaten to crush her. They threaten to destroy her very life and the light within her soul. The shadow threatens to steal her joy, her excitement, and her enthusiasm by replacing it with depression, fear, and darkness. Her light grows so faint and in the darkness she is racked with pain, misery, and tears...

...so many tears.

It's hard for me to imagine what went through her life at this point. Struggle, fear, anxiety, depression, and heart break for all that was stripped and stolen from her perfection. The darkness creeps in and becomes heavy. And she was so young. And things weren't supposed to wind up this way. And life was to be perfect. And ...

...her light wasn't suppressed completely. The imperfection wasn't so much that her perfection wasn't possible. She wasn't crushed by the shadows. She prevailed with strength, control, and patient longsuffering, looking for a day in the future, maybe even after this ever ridiculous life, that there will be a day when her imperfection becomes perfect. When this corruption puts on incorruption and becomes perfect in ways that we only see darkly as of now.

I am thirty-one years old. I ran, jumped, swam, and played with my friends in school. I am a musician, playing piano, trumpet, organ, guitar, bass, drums, and whatever else you put in front of me. I laughed, cried, and have had every experience that life can offer, both great and small. I graduated high school, graduated with a Bachelor in Mathematics, and went on to work a full-time job as a Web Developer. I am married to the real awesome person of this world, the most intelligent and beautifully designed woman that God perfectly created just for me. I am a Youth Pastor, leading a young group of great and powerful people towards a life with God.

I serve God. This is the testimony to the strength of that young girl who overcame imperfection. Her struggle is not in vain. Through my imperfection His light, power, and hand is clearly visible in my life. There is nothing I have experienced or fought through that He has not been part of and carried me through to victory, and all because of a young girl overcoming imperfection.

I am who I am because of that young girl who took on the imperfection and believed beyond perception. Ever faithful, ever trusting, and ever embedded in the arms of God, she carried this imperfection to a place where the imperfection could carry on to have a life of perfection. She prayed and prevailed, loved and patiently endured, taught and disciplined, and raised the imperfection to know that God is the only perfection. It is only through his strength that we continue, through his knowledge and love that we thrive. Our success and failures, our life and everything amazing within it, hinges completely on God, and within our imperfection, His perfection shines...

...thank you mom.

Chapter 2
The Early Years

○ ○ ○ ○ ▢

My childhood was very similar to most everyone else's except that I got sick a lot. Most kids with Cystic Fibrosis are not fortunate enough to live a life like I have lived because they are too sick to experience many things this life has to offer. Due to terrible asthma, bronchitis, pneumonia, and allergies that exacerbate breathing problems to horrific levels, most CF children do not play outside much. When I was born in 1980, a standard for CF was to do three or four long therapy sessions daily just to make sure the lungs were cleared. While this helped battle the chronic lung infections, that amount of time spent doing treatments and maintenance didn't allow for much time to play. Of course, going outside was in itself a major problem anyway for most CF children and many doctors were prescribing a life lived inside instead of exposure to harsh elements outside.

I had a bit of a difference in my childhood experience with Cystic Fibrosis. I was uber-active! In fact, I never stopped playing, running, or anything else that I wanted to do. My parents raised me a bit different from the proverbial "CF Regime" and many times were chastised for allowing me to partake in many of the more strenuous activities. As previously mentioned, many doctors at this time were prescribing a lifestyle of indoor living to help children avoid the problems associated with outdoor activities. On the surface this is great advice but reality began to paint a different picture entirely and I was not the kind of child that could be kept indoors.

My mom tells a story of when we are all sitting at the dinner table and I must have been about four at the time. I pushed my plate forward a little bit in an exaggerated fashion and proclaimed,

"I love my life."

And that was the truth. I loved life. I loved living and being alive and being active and all the other things that life brought as a child. Like many children, I had various surgeries and inevitably once I began feeling better I'd be the one who was riding the IV pole up and down the hospital floor while the nurses chased me frantically trying to keep me from killing myself. That was me. I loved life.

Some of my earliest memories are of me and my two cousins, Aaron and Melissa, playing on my grandpa's farm outside of Stigler, Oklahoma. My grandpa, like many cattle farmers, would keep large, circular bales of hay on one side of the farm and we would play on top of these hay circles. We might play hide-and-seek, tag, or any numerous imaginary games that children play. We played on them so much that my grandpa would have to get onto us just so we wouldn't end up destroying one. We also fished out of the ponds, road the tractors, road the horses, and all around did everything outside when we were at my grandparents' house. They had so much land and we spent our energy outside.

Most CF kids never go around hay. It's dusty and many times moldy and that just tears our breathing up. I remember tons of times coughing up a storm once inside the house at night but it never stopped me from going out the next morning and jumping from bale to bale and running all over that farm land.

Most of the time I was on some kind of oral antibiotics and they always caused some side effects. The most common ones are the same ones that all medicines cause which are headaches, nausea, sore throat, or something normal. Every now and then I'd have a stranger side effect that would cause trouble.

Once I was taking a medicine named Slo-Bid, or Theophylline, which is a bronchodilator. This medicine, which for me was taken by mouth, works by relaxing muscles in the lungs and also causes the lungs to be less sensitive to allergens that cause bronchospasms. I remember that I had started my first dose and then we headed out to a church youth rally. Now, aside from all the normal side effects, this medicine also produces a heightened sense of anxiety and restlessness. Basically, you get hyped up.

Church starts and of course you are supposed to sit still during the sermon. Drink five energy drinks in a row and see if you can sit still. It's impossible and this is how I felt. I remember that no matter what happened, if it was even remotely funny, I'd literally freak out laughing and literally couldn't contain myself. I was jittery and shaking all over the pew. I know the people all around me thought I was a total druggie and I'm sure they figured I was right where I needed to be considering it was church. One of the young girls sitting in the youth group section had one of those weird rolling eyeballs that go on sale during Halloween time. You know the kind that you can roll across the floor and the eye floats in water so it always looks up? Well, it accidentally fell out of her purse and went rolling down the aisle past me. Now, imagine being hyped up on drugs and seeing that during the preacher's sermon! Yeah, I literally had to leave the service because I couldn't stop from laughing. Also, my eyes were so blood shot that I am sure I resembled someone having a crazy psychotic episode.

I spent a lot of time in the doctor's offices. Whether regular doctors or specialist dealing with CF, they all knew about me. Many times we had to have checkups just to make sure I wasn't coming down with some illness, flu, or other bug that would cause my lungs to erupt in pneumonia or bronchitis. Other checkups were due to random acts of ridiculousness that seemed to follow me everywhere.

One time at my grandpas, two of my uncles decided to take me on a wagon ride. These were my mom's brothers and they were constantly fighting like brothers always do and during this wagon ride, my uncle Lyndell had thought it would be hilarious to cause the mule to run. Of course, I was pretty young at the time so this sort of scared me since I really wasn't used to wagon rides anyway seeing as I was completely citified. Well, Randall, the other brother, got mad at Lyndell and decided to take a 2X4 board and try to basically pummel him with it.

Imagine this scenario...it's truly insane.

Wagon careening out of control with a hysterical mule freaking out and Lyndell, the older brother, laughing hysterically as if there is no danger at all. The wagon then begins to run into the ditch which would ultimately cause it to tip over and eject all three of us to our deaths so Randall decides to take action by trying to smack him with a 2X4 board.

Randall winds up, aims for Lyndell's head, and swings. Lyndell, quick thinking, ducks, leaving my face directly in the line of fire. Yeah, it is like watching a cartoon, only its reality. I was like the unknowing dork that gets the brunt of the joke on this one. The board smashes me in the face on my right eye and nearly knocks my head off. Now, both boys are freaking out because I just got my brains beat out. With the cart still completely out of control, I somehow manage the courage to literally jump out of the wagon screaming. Mom comes running out, scoops me up, and takes me inside where my right eye begins to swell to the size of an apple. Fearing the worst for my eyeball, they rush me to the hospital. Everything was fine of course and I went on to be a normal child, whatever normal means.

I remember also being stepped on by a cow and being rushed to the same hospital. I'm sure the doctor there thought we were super red-necks considering the crazy stories that wound up with me getting hurt. I think in his defense, we definitely were a little crazy and I certainly know we were super red-necks.

In 5th grade I played baseball with my cousin Aaron. Our team name was the "Orioles" and we had yellow and black uniforms. I spent hours each week rolling around in the grass and dirt on the ball field, breathing in tons of dust and loving every minute. My cousin and I switched off playing first base and pitcher and I remember many games where the heat was over 100 degrees and we sweated so much we were nearly dehydrated but we loved playing baseball.

I played basketball when I was in elementary school also. I was a point guard for the "Wild Things" basketball team. I had met another boy that lived in my neighborhood and his dad was the coach and so we became friends and played ball together. In fact, I played basketball all the time, whether in an actual team setting or just loosely on the playground with friends from school and church. Almost every single day in the summer we would play ball for hours and then go swimming to cool off and then jump out and play basketball again. Ah...such a great life back in the day!

I loved everything about life except doing therapy. Ah, I hated that stuff. Yes, it was lifesaving and ultimately necessary but on a perfect day that could be spent playing ball or chasing girls, there was nothing worse than having to come in and sit with mom for a round of therapy.

Our therapy session usually followed the same ritual of mom telling me to get ready and me freaking out and whining like all kids do when they don't want to do something. Then, we'd pull out the ironing board, tilt it at around a 30 degree angle downwards, turn me upside down so that my lungs could drain downward, and mom would commence with the physical percussion therapy. This therapy, known as postural drainage, contains many different positions in which loosened secretions can be coughed out while upside down all while someone is pounding away on your body with cupped hands. They call this percussion therapy but I call it "beating your child." No, really it's not that horrible now that I look back on it but when I was a child...I hated this. We'd do a breathing treatment, followed by percussion therapy, followed by whatever other breathing antibiotic was prescribed. The hardest part was just taking the time out from a busy boy's daily life.

It's stupid. I hated it.

Sometimes dad would do the therapy and when I was younger he had this song he'd sing. Considering little boys don't want to do anything they are supposed to, anything that helped the process was definitely a miracle. The song worked too. It would go like this,

"Therapy number 1 ... therapy number 2 ... Jon David is so good..." Dad would pause here.

" ... Racoon don't know what to do!"

Then I'd bust out laughing. He included tons of animals like whales, dogs, cats, and such. They always made me laugh though and all the while he'd be beating me to a pulp with the proper chest percussion designed to dislodge mucus so that I could cough and remove the secretions. Good song, always worked.

I was blessed as a kid. I didn't have routine hospitalizations like most kids with CF. Generally, children with CF go into the hospital yearly or at least every other year but I never went into the hospital until I was 16 years old. Mostly, I attribute this to my parent's supervision and care for my CF. Daily therapy sessions using any gimmick to make me cooperate, constant attention in keeping me away from unhealthy environments, and just an overall great attitude towards the illness in general. As a kid, I really never thought of myself as a person with CF. I was just Jon and I liked to play ball, swim in the pool, and had tons of friends and activities that I loved being a part of. They never told me what I couldn't do and never kept me from trying things that they probably knew would make me sick. They always just let me try. If I could do it, then they let me keep on. If it was too much, I'm sure they helped me realize that it wasn't necessary and I'd move on.

When going into Jr. High school, I chose to join band and play the trumpet. This is a wind instrument that requires a ton of air to actually be successful to even get a note out that sounds decent. I'm sure my parents thought I was out of my mind but they encouraged me to try. I played all the way into college and even got a scholarship to a university. I remember a doctor telling me once that there was no way I'd be able to succeed in playing the trumpet but he was quick to recant considering I then informed him of my full scholarship on trumpet.

In the recent years, doctors have revised their ideas of what works with CF children. They have somewhat adopted my parents strategy of living life to the fullest that you can. They have also adopted a strategy of "no wrong way" to the approach of treatments. There is not just one course of action that works for all patients. Each is unique and will always require something different from one patient to the next, so there is no way of saying that one prescribed treatment plan is better than any other plan. To me, every plan is correct. To me, if you are trying to make it, if you are trying to battle this incredibly complex and evil disease, then you are doing the best you can, and that is the only correct approach possible. The whole idea is to improve the length and quality of life and whatever plan does that is the correct one. Of course, we know not every person can do the same things, so if you can go outside and enjoy a day, then do it. Maybe you won't get to everyday but go out on the days it's not so windy or cold. Go out on the days that it seems perfect and enjoy some sunshine. It can truly make all the difference in your world.

I've done tons of things that others with CF have never even tried. I know it's not only great parents but a great God. My reliance on God is absolute. I know that I am extremely blessed to have had parents who promoted Godly influences and lifestyles. I believe without a doubt that my childhood and the things I was allowed to experience were because God was completely sold out to keeping me healthy. Oh, I won't deny I was sick many times but prayer never failed. I don't know all that God does in our lives and I definitely don't understand everything but I know he is there and always active and I am thankful for every childhood moment.

Chapter 3
An Education Process

There is something to be said for trials and tribulation. They teach you things that otherwise you would never learn. Another thing to be said is that I wouldn't wish this learning experience on my worst enemy. It is always difficult, and always tough. I'd like to share with you a few of the smaller experiences that I've endured on the road to further education. I'll try to go in order. Probably fail.

I began being hospitalized yearly (or more) at about the age of sixteen. I don't know how old you are now but I'd like you to transport with me back in time to a section of life I'd like to title as "the most selfish period of life." This was a time when the world not only revolved around me, myself, and I, but was unable to revolve if I was not in existence. In fact, I was so important that without me the world and everything that existed would cease to exist. Intense, I know, but that was my world view at the age of sixteen, just like it was probably your view also if you were honest enough to admit it.

My first hospitalization was all about learning in the most difficult and negative way imaginable. Normally, IV medicines are introduced into the body through regular IV lines which most people are familiar with but for patients that undergo a lot of intravenous medications, other lines are used that allow medicines to be run for a longer amount of time without painful consequences to the patient. These are called "PICC Lines" and my first PICC line was lesson numero uno!

Dr. James Royall, a great and wonderful man who unfortunately had the displeasure of meeting that sixteen year old was the doctor in charge of inserting my PICC line. PICC stands for "Peripherally Inserted Central Catheter" which is a fancy way of saying that he inserted a very important and very long IV line that would be used to deliver my intravenous medicines.

They usually start with this greasy and stupid numbing cream rubbed on the area where the IV will be put. Next, they use small shots of something like Lidocaine to locally anesthetize the skin for this minor surgery. Notice the words "minor surgery." It's not just some small thing that gets put into the skin. It's "minor surgery." It evokes emotion like this:

HOLY CRAP, MINOR SURGERY!

Then the doctor begins the procedure of jamming a needle that is so big you can see the hole at the end without a microscope into the arm to find a vein. This can take a while due to the experience or lack of experience of the one doing this "finding" of the vein. Digging around and searching causes serious pain and soreness and missing veins also causes pain. To imagine the pain, take a nail and jam it into your arm. See, now you know pain! It must be noted that Dr. Royall was not inexperienced in this procedure in the least bit. He had done quite a bit of them before and even though it felt like an eternity, it was probably not.

Once found, they take a long rubbery tube that is very thin and "thread" it into the vein. This is basically pushing a rubber hose into the veins. One good thing is that once the vein is found, there isn't much pain. There is pressure and weirdness, but not pain. I really have no way of you experiencing this like the nail in the arm, so you'll just have to trust me that it is this way. I guess if you want you can shove that straw into your vein, but I advise against this, just like I advise against shoving anything into your veins. Say no to drugs kids.

This being my first time having a PICC line, I was literally freaked. The pain was new, the doctor was new, the hospital was new, that needle the size of a nail was new, and I was a punk sixteen year old who felt that everything was supposed to be perfect and pain free. Wow, what a moron I was! Nothing in the world is free kid...not even the pain.

I yelled at the doctor, told him how stupid and retarded he was, and made sure he knew that this sixteen year old thought he was completely inept and inadequate. I yelled at the nurses and nurse aides and cried and complained and carried on and basically after about 3 minutes of intense pain, and I won't lie, it was intense, I told the doctor how ignorant he was and told him to leave me alone and let me leave. I think it shocked him because he actually didn't stop digging around for that vein but instead asked me whether I was being serious. I told him he was stupid again, and yes, I was serious about removing himself from my exalted presence. Needless to say, we did not leave on good terms. And, ultimately, I had no PICC line inserted on this try.

The next day they sent in a specialist who inserted the PICC line with much the same trouble and pain but it was worse due to the previous day's torture of digging and bruising. Trust me on this when I tell you the moral of this story is short and sweet: Shut up and let them get that PICC line in the first time no matter what because by the next day your arm is in such pain that you literally want to cut it off. Don't put off today what will only torture you tomorrow. That's what I learned. Also, if you are reading this Dr. Royall, I am really sorry you met that stupid kid.

As I got older, probably closer to the age of twenty one, I had an encounter that changed me forever. It was a life lesson taught to me by a respiratory technician. They are in charge of bringing me a "breathing treatment" when I am wheezing, coughing, or short of breath. They hold the keys to comfort for an asthmatic who can't breathe well. After those breathing treatments, I feel renewed and much more comfortable. I can breathe with ease and with depth and it is so completely refreshing. These respiratory technicians are the best because they bring the medicine that enables us to breathe.

Let's call this technician in this story Chris. Chris was about six foot seven and weighed about four hundred pounds. He had a beard that resembled Santa Clause and was nearly the same age. On this particular day, he had on a red set of scrubs and black shiny boots. No kidding...I promise, I am not making this up! And he held the keys to my breathing better that morning.

Now, you have to understand, I have been doing breathing treatments at home since I was a little lizard boy. I knew how to mix the solution perfectly and on this particular day Chris was doing something weird with the mixtures. He was not measuring them correctly but instead was just pouring them in without measuring the dose. He also was breathing heavy and sweating like he'd just come out of the gym. I was a bit grossed out and immediately judged this man to be moronic at best. As he handed me the nebulizer, I realized I was going to have to educate this idiot about mixtures.

"I noticed you didn't measure out those mixtures." I began with that ever so awesome high and mighty voice that all people use at times when they know they are about to school someone.

"Yeah," he answers with a husky, breathy voice, "it doesn't really matter too much on measurements. It all goes to the same place and since you are in the hospital, the extra medication will only help."

"I've been on 0.75 milliliters of Albuterol and I don't understand how not measuring can be a good thing. It seems if I get too much medicine it could be harmful." I said in a somewhat sarcastic tone. I obviously knew better than this respiratory therapist who had probably been doing this longer than I'd been alive. At this point, things got heated real quickly. You could almost hear the tea pot whistling.

"Well, you don't have to do this breathing treatment. You can just breathe badly if you want." He was put off that I was questioning him. He was put off that I was treating him as if he was dumb.

"Well, if you aren't going to do your job correctly, then I might as well not." I was mad now. I was upset now. I was really ticked that this guy wasn't taking me seriously and was now threatening me. Who was he to take away my breathing treatment? He didn't breathe badly, although he was huffing at this point, but he had no clue as to what I felt or was dealing with. He didn't know I was the center of the universe.

It was like the meeting of two rams in the mountain. We had butted heads so quickly and severely that there was no way that we hadn't hurt each other. After butting heads, we were both so mad and stupid that we did what only could be done.

"Fine, don't do it. I don't care anyway." And with that answer, Chris, the respiratory therapist who held the keys to me breathing better, walked out of the room without administering my breathing treatment.

Lesson learned here? Don't treat people like they are stupid. If you treat people like they are stupid, then more than not, they are going to dislike you and treat you like you are stupid. This usually tends to play out where other stupid things follow, like me not getting a breathing treatment when I'm actually seriously in need of one. But, that's not all I learned in this story.

Chris returned two minutes later. He walked in, measured the amount of medicine necessary, and handed me the nebulizer. He looked at me for a second, turned on the machine, and I began breathing the mist from the nebulizer that opens my airways.

"I am sixty four years old. I do not like you but my job is to make you breathe better. I know that if you do not get this treatment, you will most likely cough and suffer. So, with that, here is the treatment measured out. Please forgive me for acting so immaturely, I shouldn't have left."

I learned. I watched a man give out mercy and kindness to someone that he didn't like. I watched and was the recipient of care and concern from a man that I had really treated poorly. This man, who held the keys to me breathing better, had been treated as an inferior person by me and was able to complete his job due to his concern for my breathing. In his intelligence, he knew that if I did not breathe that treatment, I would suffer. In that, he was unable to bring himself to leave me alone. He was unable to let me suffer just so he could be rid of me. I was a disgusting and immature thing but he came back for me to administer a medicine that I really was in need of. He was unwilling that I should suffer.

It was like an epiphany. I realized that it is not okay for someone to suffer. More than that, it is not okay to allow someone to suffer or to cause someone to suffer. Even more, it is not okay to do nothing while someone suffers. He could have left me alone in my misery, but he had compassion and brought me the very thing I needed, despite the fact that I had pretty much transgressed this man.

Suffering is not okay.

It reminded me of Jesus dying on the cross for a world that hated Him. He was in the world, the world knew him not, and not only that, but they despised and rejected Him. And yet, He had the keys to their life in His hands, and had come to save them. They spit on Him, mocked Him, and ultimately killed Him. While we were yet sinners...

Chris changed my very nature of how I dealt with nurses, doctors, respiratory therapists, and everyone in the world in general. I began a habit that very day. I made a habit of being respectful of the help. I made a habit of thanking the help. I made a habit of lavishing praise on those who brought my food, my medicines, my water, and everything else while in the hospital. But, it didn't stay in the hospital. It flowed out into every area of my life. The habit formed wrought an amazing miracle in my life. As I began, I made it a habit to say the following:

"Thank you so much. I really appreciate it."

It wasn't just a thank you. I wanted to add in the appreciative part to let the person I was addressing know that I was more than thankful and realized the sacrifice they made to help me in whatever they were doing. Guess what happened?

Hospital staff began to go out of their way to help me. By simply acknowledging and being kind, they began to move quicker, work faster, and began to want to come to my room in the hospital. I began to make friends with the staff, especially the respiratory staff. Nurses enjoyed visiting my room because they knew there was a kind and gentle person inside the room and not one that would make them suffer. Chris and I became friends. That's powerful.

I learned that kindness relieves suffering. Even in the smallest ways, if someone is suffering, a kind word of acknowledgement relieves it all. Strange that something so easy and simple isn't practiced more. I guess it is counterintuitive to our flesh. We want to prove our point. We aren't naturally patient and longsuffering when nurses don't answer our call, and then when they do, it's against nature to thank them. Thank someone for being late and slow? But here's the catch in a hospital that most people don't try to remember. Nurses have more than just you as a patient. Their work doesn't revolve around you...it revolves around ten other people who are just as sick as you. They enter rooms where people berate them all day long and take for granted their care and devotion. They are treated as morons, ignorant and inferior, and many times required to do "slave labor" that even the strongest of stomachs couldn't handle.

Then, they enter my room. They enter a kind room where they know they will not be berated and railed on, but instead will receive lavish and sincere thankfulness for their work. I remember one nurse commenting in 2009 when I was nearly dying that she had never met a kinder or more mature young man. This is the fruit of peace. It allows light to shine and is seen by all as something amazing. My favorite scripture is the one I now live by every day.

"Peacemakers who sow in peace
reap a harvest of righteousness."

It's a pride thing really. Pride causes destruction. It causes intense suffering on this planet due to people simply being so selfish. It has caused me to have difficulty in my hospital stays, mainly in my beginning years, because I was unable to see others, feel for others, and place myself in their shoes. I felt I was important and my pride nurtured suffering in both myself and the staff.

Our life isn't about ourselves but should be focused on raising another up instead of exalting ourselves. And the reward is that they see the light in us. They see the Spirit at work, they feel and know the difference. They experience the love of God through our peaceful kindness and small showering of thanksgiving. In this way, we have lifted up God. We exalt God when we exalt our brother. When we love our brother, especially in the middle of our own trials, it exalts God in ways we have yet to understand.

I dare you to try it out. I dare you to make a habit of being sincere in your thanksgiving and praise on others. It is impossible to thank people for their work and not have a return. In fact, it many times leads people to ask you about your kindness and where it originates. This leads to witnessing of the power of God, which then leads to discussions about salvation and righteousness, which ultimately leads to the salvation of a soul. Thus, the peacemaker who was peaceful and loving opened the doorway for a soul to become righteous. There is power in this scripture when we follow it, and mostly in my life, the opportunity to lavish love and care on others has been in the midst of my dark times. And therein is the power of God to take my weakness and show His strength and love. By my simple obedience of being peaceful, He is able to shine through me and reveal the truth of His abilities to others around me.

...this is the true relief for suffering.

I remember Caleb. He was six years old and drew me a picture of Spiderman and taped it to my hospital door. He was my next door neighbor in the hospital that week. He had just been diagnosed with Cystic Fibrosis and this was his first hospitalization. We'd met in the hallway while doing some exercising which is basically walking up and down the hallway. Our moms had met earlier and I said hi to him and talked a bit. We aren't really supposed to be around each other for fear of spreading or sharing bacteria that grows in our lungs. So our meeting was brief and short but during that short time we found out that he really liked Spiderman and I really liked Batman. He then placed the Spiderman picture on my door.

The first time I saw it I was a little confused. I went to the nurse station and inquired as to who put it there. They did not know. Then, after a day or so, and after quite a bit of investigation, I found out that Caleb had put it there.

And...I cried. A lot. I am a crier by nature. It's like a water faucet opens up and tears just spill out like rain drops. I cried about a great many things concerning this boy. Not just crying, but more like prayer-crying. That's when you say a few syllables to God that are unintelligible and then bawl for an hour, and then repeat that process a great many times.

I cried about the Cystic Fibrosis that would exist in his life and the depression, fear, and anxiety he would go through. I cried about the overall life that it would steal from this amazingly awesome little boy. It was like thinking about myself in a way. I looked at him, saw me, and then realized all the hardship, suffering, pain, and torment he would go through due to having an illness like this one. I prayed and cried over all the procedures, illnesses, complications, and near death experiences he'd have to battle through. I prayed and cried for his mother. Ah...there's that mother thing again. I am a super crier for sure on that one.

I learned compassion in a way I had not before and it originated from just meeting him. My heart broke immediately and I have since had the ability to look into a person instead of just at a person. I have patience to listen to their story. I have become sensitive to their needs and problems, even if they are self-inflicted, *especially if they are self-inflicted*. I see a person in their dilemma and I want to pray and cry. Caleb changed me for the better. Thanks man...Spiderman is pretty cool.

I had another habit that developed that I think wouldn't be too accepted if I made it public to my doctor. I have this habit now that when I do walk up and down the hall of the hospital, I place a hand on the doors that I pass and say a prayer. I use it as if I am laying hands on the person themselves, like I'm an Apostle or something. You learn compassion and sympathy in a hospital.

Try listening to a baby cry all night long in pain and torment, coughing and wheezing, gasping for breath and nearly dying. Try it and see what happens. You will change. Your heart will soften. You will find yourself praying and crying your face off at three in the morning that this baby would be healed immediately. All this prayer and bawling and squalling while there are no lights on, you are wearing only boxer shorts, have an oxygen line in your nose, IV line in your arm, and you yourself are wheezing and coughing, suffering from headaches and stress. You'll find yourself forgetting your own problems when you hear that baby crying. You'll find that you pray a prayer that is so amazing, so moving, and so passionate that later in your life you will remember every moment of that night, every cry of that baby, and every word you prayed to God. You will remember the realization that you never once prayed about yourself. You will learn compassion.

...try hearing that for three nights solid.

I remember watching a family. Their baby had come in extremely sick and on the verge of death. I really don't know what the problem was but I know the outcome. I remember watching the outcome. I remember watching the father and mother sitting there taking the news from the doctor. Then, I remember watching the father take a chair and ram it through the wall to where the legs broke off. I remember the noise of screaming, wailing, crying, and agony. I remember watching other items fly out of the room and watching the family struggle to find a reason. I remember the sound.

There is a sound that accompanies this specific thing. The sound is unmistakable. It's not like pain or torture. It's worse than that. In fact, tormenting pain does not have the sound that haunts you like the sound of true agony. There is no sound like that of a family member who learns their baby has passed on. I remember the sound.

There was once this nurse who had this weird attraction to me. She wasn't really a nurse but a nurse aide and she was friendly to me at first. I noticed she had a strange fascination with my illness but at first really thought nothing of it. She constantly grilled me about treatments and then that led to constant discussion about my life. I noticed the weirdness though after a while. She was really, really, really fascinated with me. After a few days I began to be uncomfortable because she would spend an inordinate amount of time in my room. It got to where even the other nurses noticed she was always in my room, always talking with me, always trying to take care of me, and eventually the nurses would have to come looking for her just to get her to do her other duties as nurse aide. I don't know what happened to her but after a few days I think she was reassigned to another floor. I learned there are weird people in this world that are attracted to strange things. Weird people who are so fascinated with a person and their illness that they literally become obsessive and feel attachment. They feel they are the only ones who can care for them in the hospital among the staff and they literally fight with other staff aides over being the one assigned to those patients. Fascinating isn't it?

Some doctors are dumb. One doctor wanted to place a PICC line in my neck. Imagine with me if you will. *An IV line in your neck.* How difficult would it be to sleep? Duh...really? Yeah, I learned that it's okay to say no to stupid.

Some nurses are not smart. I had a nurse hang the wrong IV bag. My name is always plastered on the bags that are to be used but I noticed as she hung this bag that another name was labeled on it. Obviously, I pointed this out, and she promptly freaked. No biggie...we caught it. But there is the lingering thought of "what if?" I learned paranoia.

Benadryl is your friend. Trust me on this. It's absolutely amazing. My first CAT scan revealed I was allergic to IV dye. They give you a shot of this dye that helps them see all the "stuff" better. My throat closed up, I got all itchy and hot, and started clawing at my neck. They shot me full of Benadryl and then...sleep. Glorious, holy, unblemished, perfect, and unalterable sleep. It's amazing, miraculous, and truly awesome.

They have these special nights on the pediatric floor when a specific kind of visitor comes and greets the patients. These visitors are the furry kind. They have wagging tails and wagging tongues and are always friendly. Sometimes they are dressed up in costumes but I usually feel sorry for the dogs when people do this to them. They come through usually on Thursday nights.

One time two dogs came to my door. One was dressed as Dorothy from the Wizard of Oz. They are trained in this area and really like to visit. Of course, dogs are naturally friendly and loving but it's truly amazing what happens when a dog enters the room. You can be dying in pain and agony, just have had your arm stabbed repeatedly by needles the size of nails, and then a dog enters the room, all bright eyed, tail wagging, and prancing, and it's like the world turns upside down. You sort of forget everything as you become entranced by this beautiful creation of God that is never unhappy. It's weird really. Dogs are always happy. And in a place where no one is really happy, it's pretty cool to see a dog.

I have learned many things. Many things have also been removed from my life. This process is the refining process. All the junk, anger, wrath, strife, and other character flaws that are embedded in our lives cause us to be impure. I can see now, after an education that I would never have wanted, that these trials do in fact purge us of the dross and impurities. I realize that my character is so much different, so altered by all these trials that if you took a snap shot of the character of that sixteen year old and compared it to the snapshot of my character now, the differences are staggering and amazing. I guess like Paul, in a way, I rejoice somewhat in this suffering and am thankful for the trials. That is weird to say but it is true. I look at the stupid sixteen year old and realize that God has really purged a lot of junk out of me through this process.

The entire world can tell the difference. I can look at a homeless man on the street asking me for money and immediately feel sympathy. I can go beyond feelings and actually give the man money now. I "feel" for this man. I can pray for others without ever praying for myself. In fact, I have to remember sometimes to pray for healing for myself. This was not the case for a selfish, self-centered, and egocentric sixteen year old. It wasn't even the case for the twenty-one year old. And, I won't lie, it's not natural. My education has been obtained through some very difficult trials. It has been acquired with a high price.

And, even now, I am still enrolled for the next semester.

Chapter 3.9
Short Introspection

○ ○ ○ ○ ▢

What I'm about to say is viewed through muddy, dark, and unfocused glasses. I won't explain it well, so hopefully you will just be able to "get it."

Knowing that I am part of the body of Christ, I realize that I have been called to a public ministry. I use the word public because that's just what it is. I am a Youth Pastor, which is a public, up-in-front ministry within a local assembly. All are called to private ministries but some are also used publicly.

I have been sick all of my life. I have been going to the hospital for nearly sixteen years now. I have dealt with every emotion that a person can have. I have dealt with every reaction and thought pattern associated with those emotions. I have run the gamut on every thought, action, reaction, consequence, and responsibility possible. I think there is more to this than just changing me or purifying me.

I think it revolves around ministry. In my life, if I had all that "stuff" still lingering in my character, it would be difficult to minister. I hear youth in counseling that have questions regarding life circumstances that are difficult to discuss. But, due to the things I have dealt with, the experiences and challenges I've been able to battle through and overcome with Christ, I am much better equipped. I can identify with the young person who is hurting. I can feel for the young person who is troubled. I can discuss the realities of consequences when young people make bad choices because at one point or another, I can guarantee you I have considered the same actions. I can minister in a powerful manner because I speak from experience.

In this regard, I am most thankful for the "stuff" that has been purged from my character. If I didn't know how to deal with "life", I'd be a very bad minister, unable to identify and understand. I believe that God has brought me through the fire so that I can help bring others through the fire. In the end, we will be pure, and even though it really hurts, I am thankful to know Christ and participate in his suffering.

Chapter 4
Never More Than I Can Bear

○ ○ ○ ○ ▢

Imagine with me if you will...

Sixteen years old. Can you remember when you were sixteen? Are you sixteen? Are you headed towards sixteen? Are you still acting sixteen? Threw that in for comical effect. This section is integral to understanding the background of some of the earlier stories of my life. Don't get mad at me because I told you I wouldn't go in chronological order.

Sixteen year old boys are basically crazed and emotionally freaked out kids striving for a grasp on any kind of reality. Hormones race, hearts pump, and everything revolves around girls. They are encountering for the first time independence from parents, from home, and from even the foundations of their upbringing. They are striking out on their own, blazing their own trails, all the while under the blessed wings of God who basically puts His hand on them so they don't kill themselves.

In the summer before my senior year of high school, that description would sum up my state of being. I had grown up in the church like so many other children who slept underneath the pews while pastors preached the wonderful sermons of church. I was one of those children playing with toys as a toddler while the pastor waxed eloquent on scripture. I was that kid in the church whose parents were teachers, preachers, and leaders. I was that kid. I was a preacher's kid in a way.

Dad was the role model. He was the father who taught the importance of going to church, of faithful attendance, and was a local preacher invited to speak on many occasions around the local churches. He was an accomplished musician with talent above and beyond most other musicians. With abilities in teaching, preaching, leading, and music, my Dad was heavily used in the ministry both publicly among the congregation and privately at home as a role model to me during my childhood. He was the leader of the Sunday school class that I attended at our church when I was a teenager and became a mentor and counselor to many of the young people that came through his classroom.

Dad was a spiritual leader and the lessons I learned still stick with me even today. Lessons on giving, on devotion, on separation, and on every other conceivable thing you can expect a spiritual leader to teach to both a Sunday school student and a son. His knowledge of the Bible was gained through attending Bible School in Jackson College of Ministries, both in classroom studies and in personal studies. I am blessed to have inherited his curiosity for scripture.

Imagine being the son of that man. Imagine watching for years the Spirit move through his words and music. I'm certain this was a major reason why I became a musician and student of God. I watched the blessings fall onto that man in the form of a loving family, awesome job opportunities and promotions, important church positions, and gifts handed over directly from God. I saw the benefit of giving, the benefit of devotion to the church, and God poured out untold blessings on that man in ways that are unbelievable. He was the foundation. He was the first teacher. He was the leader in the home and the first role model of that sixteen year old boy.

At age sixteen though, the foundation failed. It cracked and fell away from the house causing significant structural damage.

The foundation that had been so solid and so dependable washed away and became sand underneath my feet. It's like when the ocean water crashes on the shore and the sand you are standing on is swept away and you begin to sink. It's like blindness so dark and confusing that you are literally at a loss for words, actions, or even emotions. It's numbness at the realization that your life has changed forever.

I watched my father fall into sin and take a course of action that was absolutely against God, and it crushed me. It confused my logic, reasoning, and beliefs. The man who taught me to always seek God, seek righteousness, and seek truth was now seeking something else. My life reeled out of control for a little while and the repercussions have had some serious consequences.

That summer was tough. Depression, fear, anxiety, and all that great stuff that came rushing into the dramatic life of an already overly stimulated and hormonally imbalanced sixteen year old nearly drove me crazy. How are you to deal with a situation where your life-long beliefs are in question? Was God even real? Were any of those lessons legitimate? What about all that living for God business and the commitment business and the church devotion and all that? What about truth and righteousness? What about everything?

The answer for that summer came in a strange way. I was sent to Louisiana Youth Camp to work through their entire camp season. I worked in the kitchen among other youth for five weeks solid in the month of July, in the year of 1997, a month before I turned seventeen. It was a foundational experience.

Searching for answers, I sought God in a godly environment surrounded by godly people. I was surrounded by God in the form of new friends who served Him and youth ministers who were using their talents to create a spiritually awesome environment for young people.

One such man was Clifton Lejeune. He took me in under his wings and watched over me as chaperone. He directed me, prayed with me, spoke with me, counseled me, and overall took over as a spiritual leader that summer. I remember he was so involved that even during the wild services where God was moving in a powerful way, and even though he was part of the officiating crew responsible for governing the entire camp season, he would be constantly aware of me, constantly aware of whether I was responding to God, of whether I was praying, and of my every motion.

He "watched" me as if his life depended on it. He "directed" me in the ways of approaching God when in need of serious direction and guidance as if I was his own son. He pushed me and provoked me to a realization that God is so much more than just lessons and static theology. He helped me to truly experience God. His wisdom was amazing and I am in debt to this man in so many ways. He forced me to seek God and find Him. That summer was a restructuring of a foundation that had torn away at the seams. The spiritual ramifications of that summer will never be fully understood until we are in eternity and God is able to open our understanding of what really happened to me. That's the power of a truly devoted man of God, sold to the concept of ministering to this world and willing to do whatever is necessary so that others can know God. I am eternally thankful for Cliff Lejeune and the time he took to love and care for a young person that was hurting and confused. I love you man...and yes, you are the craziest person I have ever met.

I spent five solid weeks in that atmosphere of powerful, spirit-filled classes and services. I spent five solid weeks with Godly, spirit-minded men and women. I learned about spiritually inspiring music like Kirk Franklin that literally changed my outlook on Christian music as a whole. Before Kirk, Christian music was dull, lifeless, and ultimately boring in my ears. But with Kirk, I realized that Christian music can have a beat, can contain more than cheesy and shallow lyrics, and can actually be awesome. I remember they played "Stomp" during a day session and everyone in the audience went nuts and started dancing and worshipping all at the same time. I'd really never seen that before. Oh, I'd seen worship and dancing, but I was not accustomed to people just doing this for no other reason than to have fun. It was a learning experience that opened my eyes to a very different concept of just what it was to worship God with our being. I know some don't agree with what I'm about to say, but I learned that it is okay to dance and enjoy "church". I learned that it was okay to get into the worship service, even if I felt like doing nothing. I learned the "physical" side of worshipping God.

I can be honest with you, I didn't feel like worshipping. I really didn't feel much of anything when I first arrived. I knew there were major problems within my family and I was struggling with confusion about God in general. It weighed me down. But after the first class, after the first experience of the rejuvenating and restoring power that God pours out on those that seek him when in desperate need, I couldn't help but dance, shout, sing, and praise. It would have been out of place to not allow God to do all that he was doing, even though I may not have understood everything going on in my life or even in that camp season.

I remember three and four hour altar experiences. I remember friends praying with me so seriously. They spoke with me, listened to me, and cared for me, even though we had never met before that season. I was blessed to have those friends at that camp. Somehow God had miraculously matched me in the kitchen crew with musicians, singers, and serious worshippers. In the services, sitting in the midst of those types of people who were not intimidated or embarrassed to sweat for God in their worship, I learned and experienced things unlike ever before. And I did worship. I shouted and danced for God nightly and laid it all out on the altar. I cried and bawled for hours on end and poured out my troubles onto the shoulders of the God who can carry every care.

I gave it all to Him and it healed me. It restored my faith in God. It rejuvenated my Spirit and reshaped what it means to walk by faith. My strength is in Him and even though I may be weak and completely without control, God will be there, He will raise a standard up against the flood and will be the mighty fortress and strong tower.

I came home after this spiritual high as sick as possible and went directly into the hospital for the first time in my life, the horrible events of which you have already read about. There's that "out of chronological time" that I warned you about. My Dad separated from my Mom and moved out of the house a week after I returned home from the hospital, which was a week before my senior year of high school. Trust me when I tell you, it was a lot to bear as a sixteen year old. Senior year is such big deal to a teen and it's supposed to be awesome, fun, and happy, but mine was not. I went into that school year knowing my Dad was gone.

I believe without a doubt that if I had not spent a season with God like I had just experienced, I would have most likely lost it all, both mentally and spiritually. Without the reparation of faith that I had received from that summer, the events of my father leaving home before my senior year of school would have toppled me.

The stress and trauma of my first hospital visit coupled with the tumultuous and faith destroying consequences of a family that was dissolving is impossible to truly convey to anyone who has never gone through that kind of fire. Pair that with the fact that at sixteen years old, life in general seems overwhelming at best. I know that without that summer of Louisiana camp, I would have failed. I would have given up on God. But when I arrived home, realized the immensity of the family situation, and encountered my first hospital nightmare, I faced it with a strange certainty that would not have been there had I not just been on the mountain in the presence of the Almighty.

I had destroyed many lions and a few bears upon those altars during that entire five week season, so I could defeat these giants also. I could withstand this pressure also. I could overcome this situation also because what was in me was greater than anything this world could ever bring against me.

No weapon could destroy me. I was accompanied by the Almighty, the King of Kings, the Lord of Lords, and the one perfect, loving, and powerful God who spoke it all into existence in the beginning. That was my God and he would supply my needs, be my strength, and carry me through this storm.

Chapter 4.8
The Rest Of The Story

○ ○ ○ ○ ☐

And now ... the rest of the story. I encourage you to never give up hope. I encourage you to never give up prayer, devotion, and commitment to God. Remember that our faith is not in men, but in God, the creator and supplier of all things.

God works in ways I do not understand and I don't really need to understand. He is God and I am not. I trust in Him with my life and place my all in His hands. I follow Him and live for Him above all other things. And I have never seen the righteous forsaken.

My father lived in sin for years doing things absolutely contrary to the way I was raised. But God wasn't through with him. He has since come back to God. He has since rejoined the faith. He now lives for God along with a wife that might not have found God had it not been for his falling away. He serves God in their local assembly with an even stronger and stricter devotion than before. Our relationship has been restored also in an even more loving and intimate way. This is the power of God.

I include this part of the story because it is vital to our faith. We must believe our loved ones will come back to God. We must trust in God enough and realize that there is no sheep that is beyond the far reaching hand of God. The Psalmist wrote in

Psalm 139 that there was nowhere he could travel that he could not escape God. Even making a bed in hell, following after sin and debauchery, and even running from God, there is still no way to escape Him. He is everywhere and he loves everyone so much.

The perception is that God's love is limited. The perception is that God won't love us. The perception is that God will reject us. The perception is that God, based on our life, can't save us, because we perceive our actions or lives to be so heinous and disgusting in God's sight that he will spew us away from his presence with contempt and judgment.

How could God love us? We sin willfully and arrogantly in his face, mocking him and crucifying him anew with each selfish action. How could God love me? Why would he want a damaged, tired, or worn out life, ruined by situations and circumstances either controlled or uncontrolled? Why would he want to be around me, and be interested in my life? How could God love me, a person who has delved in a lifetime of evil? The reality is this and only this. Listen to me right now. Don't get distracted. This is the reality and this is the only reality.

If I make my house in hell, if I dwell there, sleep there, eat there, and engage myself in the pleasures in hell, God is always there. You may have lived in hell all of your life, enjoying the splendors of the lust of the eye, lust of the flesh, and the pride of life but know this one thing that God is there and he has been there the entire time. While you created for yourself a habitation surrounded by the spiritual evils of hell, he's been there. It may have been your home for years, or in some cases, your entire life since you've been able to distinguish what sin really is but there is one thing we have to remember.

There is nowhere that God can't go. You can run to the furthest reaches of the Earth to escape him but you will fail. You may, as the Psalm indicates, try to flee his presence, but as it asks so plainly: Where will you go to escape God? He is infinite, boundless, and timeless. There is nowhere that God cannot go, nowhere that God cannot be, and nowhere that God cannot walk right into because he created it all. And as a creation, we are subject to that master. We are subject to that God.

God loves us. If we make our bed in hell, he loves us enough to sleep there with us. If we ascend to the highest heights of the world, even ascending into heaven itself, he's there, loving us and standing right beside us. If we sail to the end of the Earth, we won't escape his love. And even as we sail away, he holds us in his arms! Even there in the bed of hell and sin and death and chaos his arms surround us and his hands lead us. He loves us so much that he leads us even while we are running from him because there is no one that has ever been born, no one that has ever sinned so much that he doesn't want them. There is no life that is so destroyed, no life that is so messed up, no life that is so out of control, no life that has gone through so much, that he doesn't want them.

God came to seek and save that which was lost. Even those things running from him, climbing the highest mountains, hiding in caves, sailing to the furthest reaches of the Earth, buried beneath the sands of a lifetime of hurt and suffering. They are all lost sheep, running scared, helpless, and without direction but all being followed, pursued, and sought by the LORD, by the God of all creation, by the true shepherd of all life.

Even if you are being devoured by lions, by the sinful spirits of this world, and only have pieces of a broken life, maybe just a leg or a piece of an ear, God will reach into the very mouth of those demons, the very mouth of those lions, and not only retrieve your broken, scarred, and destroyed pieces, but he'll recreate you better than you were. He will make you a new creation, a new life, born again of his power, his Spirit, and his love, free of the bondage and destruction of the sinful lifestyles this world has to offer and free of the scars of suffering.

There is no one he does not want. There is no one he will not save. There is no one that he will not set free. There is no one he does not seek after to save for we were all lost, we were all sinners and while we were yet sinners, Christ died to seek and to save that which was lost.

So don't count your loved ones out. Faithfully pray and seek God for their restoration to this faith. There is no person who has sinned so much that God cannot save. And there is no one, no matter the condition, the scars, the guilt, shame, turmoil, or chaos that God does not love and want. Why?

For he came to seek and to save that which was lost.

I love my Dad so much. Our relationship and the ability to discuss the things of God openly is refreshing. His renewed Spirit and dedication to God along with a devoted wife is amazing and miraculous and it is inspiring. I do not understand all the complexities that this type of plan required but I do cherish the results.

Chapter 5
Short Story Time

○ ○ ○ ○ ▢

That One Homeless Guy

When I was in college, I lived at home with my Mom and Stepfather. Their room was upstairs and mine was downstairs connected to a small half bathroom that contained a toilet and sink. One time when I was on high doses of pain killers after one of my sinus surgeries I had an encounter with a homeless man.

I had taken quite a dose of pain killers after my sinus surgery that you'll encounter later in the book. Now remember, I told you not everything would be straight forward, so just trust me when I tell you that the sinus surgery caused some major pain. So, I took pain pills.

That night while sleeping, I happened to wake up somewhere in the middle of the night to see a homeless man pushing one of those shopping carts through my bedroom. He looked exactly like all stereotypical homeless men that typically walk through your bedroom in the middle of the night. His cart was all creaky and he had on a trench coat and pretty much looked the part of any normal homeless guy. He pushed his cart, which of course had those weird plastic sacks with stuff in them into the bathroom that was connected to my room, turned the light on, and closed the door.

About a minute later, I saw a shaggy white dog resembling a floor mop go tromping through my room following this homeless man. The bathroom door opened, the mop dog went in, and the door closed.

Now, normally when someone invades your bedroom in the middle of the night it evokes fear and chaos because home invasion doesn't normally feel good. But, I was on high doses of pain killers and my feelings were somewhat numb and out of balance. So, me being the courageous one, I just sit there staring at the bathroom door. I couldn't quite figure out why that guy and his dog were in my bathroom. I knew they were there though because the light was on, shining through the bottom of the door.

I got up slowly and hesitantly moved ever closer to the bathroom door. I couldn't hear anything in the bathroom so I feared I would startle the homeless man and his mop dog. In silence, without startling the homeless guy, I slowly opened the door and stuck my head in. Immediately, I regretted my choice of action.

I did not find a homeless man or a mop dog in my bathroom. Instead, what I found was a floor, walls, and ceiling covered with cockroaches, desperately trying to find a hiding place away from the light. They were everywhere crawling on the sink, the walls, the toilet, and the cabinet. They were literally swarming the small bathroom and there were so many cockroaches that I couldn't even see the floor. Instead, all I saw was moving bugs everywhere.

So I did the most obvious thing that all of us would do in a situation where a random homeless man and his mop dog had just infiltrated my bedroom and then been replaced by a bathroom full of cockroaches. I promptly got back in bed and went sound asleep. The next morning I recounted my story to my Stepfather and alerted him to the idea that our bathroom was overrun with cockroaches. My Mom knew immediately I had hallucinated and that was the end of that story.

This Is For Tyler

Tyler is one of the most recently licensed nurses on the pediatric floor where I have been visiting for the past few years. He's very cool, very awesome, and very intelligent, which is why this story is so funny. I am honored to have him as a friend and especially grateful to him and all the other nurses on the 10th floor at Baptist. You are all amazing and truly a blessing from God. You are angels encamping round about them that are in pain and you are magical in every way. Did I butter you up enough?

One night, Tyler was changing my lines out. Typically, this is done weekly or every four days and it fell on his shift to perform this task. On this night, he was already kind of tired and so he came in to my room ready with all the bags and new lines to change but forgot the saline. We are very casual in my room and tend to cut up and laugh. My room is also the "get away" room for nurses who have been yelled out, cussed out, or just stressed out. Sometimes they will just walk in my room, close the door, stand there for about two minutes, not really say much, and then head back out to the chaos that is a pediatric floor shift.

Tyler heads back down the hall to get saline. He shows up at my door again, begins to change the lines, and realizes he forgot the caps that go on the ends. So, he walks back to the nurse station, gets the caps, and returns. He begins to flush the line, attempts to hook the end of the saline to the IV, but it doesn't quite connect. So, as he flushes the line, which is basically just pushing saline through to clear out any leftover medicines, the saline pours out all over my lap. So, he has to get more saline, considering he just poured out what he had brought on my crotch. He connects the line very well and secure this time, flushes the line, and continues to hang the medicines.

In changing the TPN line, a nutritional medicine that makes me gain weight, he ends up pouring much of it all over the floor and on my bed. Now, this stuff stinks like vinegar. Then, after getting everything cleaned up and hooked up, he begins to walk out of the room, feeling all is well and connected. Which it was except for the fact that he had forgotten to actually start the infusion pump.

Nice one Tyler! We laughed for a long time and he said, "I'm glad you know me." I'm glad I know Tyler. He is one of many nurses that make a horrific stay bearable and sane. And trust me, laughter is a great medicine!

Dr. Flux

My first Doctor was named Dr. Flux. He was a retired four-star general who had served in the military and had not fully realized he wasn't still in the military. His mannerism, his character, and his rather brisk and aggressive approach at the bedside was all about the military mindset. He barked an order and the nurses and technicians jumped and ran, already answering too late in his mind. My mother tells me he was not the nicest man she had ever met and on more than one occasion had received an ever-famous tongue lashing.

However, for some strange reason, the man loved me. He would come into the clinic, riled up and ready to destroy the enemy, and then melt around me, spending tons of time talking and laughing with me. In fact, he would feed me breakfast.

Yes, you read that correctly. A four star general would feed me breakfast every morning during one of my times in the hospital. This time in the hospital was for a normal surgery and not like a typical CF visit but still, my doctor would come up to my room after probably making some nurse aide cry and turn ' into a ball of mush and feed me breakfast.

It is so strange how some people are and how they react to different people. Of course, I had no clue at all that he was a four-star, decorated general. I was so young I barely remember anything about him but I am told he always melted around me.

More About Nurses

Rayla brought me a fork in the middle of the night when I couldn't breathe well and couldn't really walk down the hallway. This is not a small event and I will not forget it. Nurses aren't waiters and waitresses but she was willing to help me. That is something that matters to me and I do not take it for granted.

Kevin took some candy out of a big candy bag I had while in the hospital and then asked if he could have some. This was truly funny because as he was stealing my candy, he asked if he could have it. The funny part was that he realized the humor and we laughed for quite a while. He says,

"Can I have this candy that I'm stealing?" Of course it cracks me up. He continues,

"Guess it would be awkward now if you said no." Oh man, we laughed. Yes, you may not understand why it is so funny but at 2am on Benadryl while your oxygen is basically awful and you feel like you are dying, things tend to be very funny.

Kristen always has the terrible task of changing my PICC line dressing. Basically, it's this super adhesive tape that holds the PICC line in place and it has to be removed, the skin underneath cleaned with alcohol, and then a new super adhesive tape is replaced, all in the effort to keep things clean, sterile, and infection free. Unfortunately, this task always seems to fall on her.

I moan and groan while she torturously removes the tape and then she takes the alcohol and literally rubs it all over the PICC line insertion point. Yeah, basically pour alcohol in a wound and that is what it feels like. I realize it's necessary but seriously!

I want to state here and now that she is awesome at removing tape, excellent at torture, and I appreciate her work. Maybe someone else will change my next PICC line dressing but if not, I'm good with you!

The twins are a pair of nurses that are sisters and they do look exactly alike. I can usually tell the difference due to hair styles and such but many times they like to help each other out through the daytime. One visit will be with one and then about thirty minutes later, the other twin will come in and do something else. It's very confusing and many times I want to comment but I fear I might call them by the wrong names. So, I just watch and feel like I'm in the Twilight Zone. You never know...luckily they are both really good at what they do so I never worry. But, I do feel like I'm in another universe...

Sharks In My IV Lines

This is one of my favorites. It will be yours as well. Or else I'll punch you in the face.

One time while in the hospital, I had a dream. This is a very violent and deranged dream so if you are young, avert your eyes immediately. Maybe you ought to ask your parents if you are old enough to read this mentally messed up dream.

I was sitting up in the hospital bed. That's how this dream starts. The hospital beds electronically move up and down allowing people to lay back or sit up with ease and I was in the sitting position. As I begin to observe my IV line, I notice that in the little bags of medicine, there are sharks swimming around. Now, these are small sharks and they are just casually swimming around in a circle like normal sharks do. I feel a little tense about this but nonetheless I try not to let it bother me.

A nurse comes in and begins the pump that starts the medicine running into my IV line and I immediately notice that the sharks are now one by one swimming into the line and exiting down towards my IV insertion site. Each shark starts heading down the line and there is about one foot between each one that enters the line. I am a little more tense and nervous about this and try to tell the nurse that there are sharks in my IV line but she tells me that she can't see them and leaves the room.

As the sharks move down the IV line, I notice they start to grow into real life-size sharks. I am now very tense and nervous, frightened that the sharks are going to enter my veins and cause me severe pain since they are growing too big to fit. I mean, come on, my veins are only so big and these sharks are growing at a very rapid rate. By now, there are close to ten sharks slowly making their way down the IV line.

I push the nurse call button because at this point I am a little frantic. I'm sweating and nauseated due to the inclement danger that is so obvious and as my nurse comes in to see what the problem is the first shark in the line gets very close to the IV insertion site. I unhook the IV from my arm and hold it out towards the floor because at that very instant a shark has now fully arrived in full size at the end of the tube. Still, the nurse is acting like nothing is wrong which causes me severe stress.

The shark flops out onto the floor along with a lot of fluids and begins sort of swimming around on the floor with its mouth constantly chomping open and closed. Other sharks are now flopping out onto the floor and splashing around in the fluid that has now spilled all over the floor. The sharks are obviously starving because they start swimming towards the nurse and begin shredding her into bits. Blood and flesh pieces are flying everywhere and it looks like a frenzy that you'd see on Shark Week. There is so much blood that the fluid in the room thickens and turns blood red.

Finally all of the sharks flop out of the IV line and start to swim down the hallway devouring patients and nursing staff leaving a trail of bloody flesh pieces all over the walls and floors. The sharks make their way to the nurses' station where they begin to literally eat the entire station, computers, medicines, and everything else that exists. And for whatever reason, everything bleeds tons of blood. It's like fountains of blood just flowing out of each desk, computer, monitor, or chair that the sharks have torn into. It was really overkill of course but hey, it's a dream.

I remember in the dream feeling helpless and the whole entire thing had that truly nightmarish feel to it that makes us wake up in a sweat. It was a rough dream but I realize now it was probably due to some stupid medicine I was on at the time.

Or was it?
(mysterious music as we fade out)

The Devil Drawing

In the middle of the night I awoke and was looking around my room and noticed a nightmarish devil picture. It was red with horns and a tail and a pitchfork. I remember feeling slightly concerned that there was a devil drawing in a pediatric floor but of course went back to sleep.

The next morning I looked at the drawing a bit closer to find it was actually a goat dressed as a farmer with a shovel. Some kid had colored it and left it on the wall. Interesting how the mind changes things when we're on drugs.

The Radio Flyer

When I'm in the hospital, it is always a great help to have friends come and visit. A normal visit consists of friends coming up to the hospital and they sometimes bring food. One of my coworkers always brings me a pot roast potato from City Bites which just happens to possibly be the best food on the planet. Thank you Cato!

We tend to cut up and laugh and those visits help to pass the time. They also help us because they are encouraging and uplifting and help my wife and I get our minds off of the obvious negative feelings that we have during times of trouble in the hospital.

During one visit, we were sitting around and laughing like normal when all of a sudden my friend, Stephen Dearman, went across the hallway and brought in one of those play wagons that are red and typically have the "Radio Flyer" title on the side. They aren't very big and most of the nursing staff uses them to pull their small children patients around during times when they feel okay to get out of the room and get exercise.

Something I might should point out is that I am always put on a pediatric floor. No matter what hospital I've been to and no matter how old I get, I am always on the pediatric floor, so these wagons are not out of place considering little children can use them for fun and playtime.

Well, my friend Stephen decides he wants to pull me around the hospital floor. Now, I am 30 years old. I am 5'8" and weigh around 130 pounds. I am not a child and I am not nearly as small as those children that typically get pulled around in those Radio Flyer wagons. All of this seems to have escaped my friend and quickly escapes me because in a moment of sheer retardation, I jump into the wagon, we position the IV pole in front of the wagon, and he begins to pull me around the floor.

Let me say it out loud: Large adult male, 5'8" in height, around 130 pounds last seen being pulled by another adult male in a Radio Flyer wagon on the pediatric floor of the hospital.

We went by other kids in their Radio Flyer wagons and I'm sure they were thinking, *How old is that kid? And wow...he's really big for a child.* No kidding.

Of course, we had a great laugh and had a ton of fun and even got some ever embarrassing pictures from the whole thing that were promptly posted on Facebook for the world to see. I will never forget that wagon ride. I'm sure the nurses and staff and children on the floor won't forget seeing that obviously mentally handicapped child, who for some reason was really big and bearded, being toted around by that helpful man. Oh the things you see in a hospital.

The Prison Inmate Next Door

Yes, I have had a prison inmate next door. Well, not "literally" next door, but three doors down. I think that's close enough to be considered basically next door. So, let me start over. Yes, I have had a prison inmate three doors down from my hospital room during one of my visits.

At first I wasn't sure what it was. I saw it walk down the hallway escorted by four very large police officers but it was like watching a scene from the Green Mile. The inmate was literally larger than all four put together. And these weren't your typical scrawny drug store cops. These were those 6'6" mammoth correctional officers whose biceps look like basketballs and who wear tires for sweat bands around their wrists. It was those kinds of guys but the inmate was literally dwarfing them all.

It was like watching a bear walk in the midst of four very small shrubs. Towering over them in height, weight, and width, this man was one of the biggest men I have ever seen in real life. Oh, we've watched those movies with massive men but it's a completely different experience watching the Incredible Hulk live and in action. Of course, he was just walking down the hall but they had him in leg and arm shackles and these officers all had batons out. They were not just armed with batons at the sides of their belts...no, these batons were actually out.

Something about that gave me a chill but I figured if there had been a real threat I'd have known when I began being eaten alive by the bear-monster-inmate three doors down.

A Special Christmas Gift

For Christmas 2010, my wife Sallie and I decided to visit her family that lives in Orlando, Florida. Christmas time in Florida is so amazing because it's not cold but almost perfect weather. Her father and step mother live on a lake and it's just a beautiful place to visit. Sallie and her father love Disney World which is only about fifteen minutes from the house and so there is just a great wealth of adventure just waiting to be explored.

One day during this particular Christmas vacation, we all decided to go shopping at one of the outdoor malls. The day was perfect with little wind and everyone seemed to be having a great time. At about noon time, I received a phone call.

"This is the Oklahoma City Police Department calling to talk with Jonathan Sacker. Is this Jonathan Sacker?" This was the introduction on the phone call.

"Yes," I replied "this is him."

"Mr. Sacker, we have been trying to contact you regarding your home. There has been an accident and we need to find out what you would like us to do." The officer continued.

"What kind of accident?" I asked. By now I'm convinced my house has burned down. That's about the only thing I could think of that would warrant such an ominous phone call.

"Well, the accident is a little different because there was a car that smashed into your garage door. After this, a woman got out of the car, went through a small hole that had been created from the collision, and then about three minutes later, came out and left." The officer finishes.

"What?" I ask with that tone that nearly everyone uses when they absolutely have heard something crazy. "Is this a joke?"

"No sir," the officer sort of laughs, "this is definitely not a joke though it sounds a little funny. The woman seems to have been high on spray paint because we found a number of cans that had spilled out of her car as she exited to go into your garage."

"Did she steal anything?" I ask now in a haze of unreality due to such a crazy story.

"Well, it doesn't seem so. It seems she just went in the garage and then couldn't decide what to do so she just came back out and left. We viewed some security footage from one of your neighbors that shows her careening into your driveway and then smashing into your garage door. Luckily, she did not go in the house." He again sort of laughs.

"So you are telling me that a crazy lady smashed through my garage and then left all while being high on spray paint and that you saw it all on my neighbor's security camera? Did you arrest her?" I ask now beginning to think like the crime scene investigator that I know I should have been.

"No, we couldn't get a clear image of the car tag. She drove off before anyone had a chance to stop her. We probably won't find her either." He replies. "It does look like the garage door smashed into your cars and motorcycle though. The bike looks pretty scratched up."

Nail in the coffin.

My motorcycle was scratched up. Ah...this was a tragedy of biblical proportions. And to top it off, they hadn't been able to arrest her so that would leave it all up to me and my own insurance to fix any problems that had been caused to my two cars and one motorcycle that had been slammed by the garage door.

But that wasn't it. The officer continued on with even better news about the garage door.

"Because the door has a huge gap it leaves the house insecure. We can't leave the house like that because someone could gain access to the inside so you'll have to authorize someone to replace the garage door immediately."

Okay, I'm in Florida. I'm on vacation during Christmas time and we just finished spending money shopping and now I'm told I have to buy a new garage door basically that day to secure my home that is in Oklahoma City. Guess how much that was? Guess how difficult it is to find someone to install a brand new garage door the week of Christmas without notice? Guess how much my deductible was? Yeah, so I bought a brand new garage door for Christmas because some crazy, spray paint sniffing, psycho hose beast decided to smash into my house. Thanks for that one.

In all, the bill was around $800 bucks and that's without ever getting any car fixed. On the car front, each separate vehicle also had a deductible so you can see how it all added up fairly quickly. Greatest Christmas present ever and I still haven't bought new pipes for my motorcycle. I just love the smashed up, scratched up vintage look that I now have. So groovy.

Best part though of the whole story is the fact that this woman had two kids in the back seat of her car. In the security video you could clearly see two small figures in the backseat probably freaking out as their mother crashed into some house and then got out. Since it was Christmas week, I really think she had planned to steal Christmas presents. There ought to be some sort of way to stop people like her from procreating. It's just sad.

I Am Tarzan

One day when I was a teenager I decided to try to be Tarzan. I don't know if you watched Tarzan as a kid but he was most known for swinging through the forest on vines and constantly yelling. On this particular day in my life, I had decided to also try this amazing feat.

We lived in a neighborhood that had a creek that flowed behind our house and it was your usual creek with large boulder rocks in it and very little water unless it rained. If it was raining, then it was a very wide and dangerous rushing creek which every now and then some kid would get caught in and usually end up very badly. But on this day, the creek was normal with a low amount of water.

I had tied a twine rope to the bridge that went over the creek in the thought that I would swing from one side of the creek bank to the other. The creek bank itself was about three feet taller than the water line on either side so swinging from one side to the other should have not involved me ever getting wet. Greater than that, it would look so cool!

Imagine with me if you will. Jonathan Sacker, man of the wild, swinging fearlessly on a twine rope "vine" and bellowing loudly with power and poise making all the other inferior creatures envious. This is exactly what I imagined as I tied the rope to the bridge and backed up on one side of the creek bank in preparation for my daredevil flight.

I took a running start, pulled the rope tight as possible in order to swing across, and went airborne...for about one whole second. At the point that the one whole second passed, the twine rope snapped completely and I went sailing back first into the creek bed. In the creek were boulders literally the size and weight of myself at that age that could have easily killed me instantly if I had slammed against them with my head or back. I went hurtling at a very fast pace directly at them and somehow miraculously landed in the muddy, shallow water in the middle of four or five of these huge rocks. The mud literally padded my crash and miraculously I didn't dash myself on any of the rocks. The water was so low that only my back got completely wet but I did end up with mud nearly everywhere on my clothes, hair, and body.

The strangest thing is that the only thing I could think of was that I would have to take a shower because it was a Wednesday and we would be going to church that night. I laid there in the muddy water for a little bit and some of my friends that had witnessed this fiasco tried to help me out of the water. I think they thought I had died.

I slowly crawled out of the creek and up the bank to drier ground and then up the small incline onto the neighborhood road. I had the beginnings of about a million bruises, cuts, and scrapes and so I began the small but very difficult walk back to my house. It was only about ten houses away but it seemed like an eternity as I hobbled along, drenched with water and mud, feeling like my body was on fire with aches.

I went in the house and my mom was sitting in the living room. I didn't even say hi to her but instead just kept slowly hobbling down the hall into the bathroom. I stripped off all my clothes and got in the shower. After about five minutes I hear the bathroom door being knocked on.

"Jon, are you okay?" My mom can't figure out why her son just came in and got in the shower without a word.

"Yeah, I'm fine." I lie. My arms, legs, and everywhere was completely sore, scratched, and hurting.

I hear the door open and of course my mom sees a muddy mess of wet clothes everywhere on the floor. After the shower, I dry off, put some pajamas on and just climb into bed. She comes in and of course I recount the awesomeness of my Tarzan scenario. She gives me something to relax my muscles since they are completely hurting and bruised and the rest was just history.

It really was a miracle that I didn't break my back or neck. God must have been watching that stupid kid trying to swing across the creek. I never tried it again.

Motorcycle Mayhem

In 2009 I decided that it was time to step up and be a man. Now, to be a man requires a number of things but most notably it requires a house with a grill. Added to that list is a motorcycle which is what I purchased in 2009.

My motorcycle is a Yamaha V-Star with pearl white finish. It is basically the most awesome looking motorcycle on this planet and I love it! I had not originally been looking for a pearl white motorcycle but it has since become my favorite color for any motorcycles. My wife also loves the color which added I think to the reason I bought that particular one.

Now, I need to give you some background. I know nothing about vehicles. If the oil gets changed in my car, it's because of someone at Wal-Mart. On the subject of motorcycles though, I am even less informed. I had never ridden a motorcycle before the day that I bought one. I know, I'll go ahead and say it for you because I know you are thinking it.

Wow, that is just stupid.

Well, yes it may be "just stupid" but I'm telling you that motorcycle is awesome and I was not concerned with the fact that I might bash my brains out on the concrete just trying to sit on it. And, just so you know, I had thought ahead and brought my friend Tim Warren who actually could drive a motorcycle so that he could drive it home for me. So there...ha! Showed you.

Once home and safely in my driveway, I began the process of learning how to drive a motorcycle. I took about three days just sitting in my driveway giving it gas and barely moving forward. I would then brake, back up, and do it all over again in order to get used to taking off. I really didn't want to wreck my beautiful motorcycle so I probably was overly cautious. I finally did take off, staying in first gear rolling down the road slowly and proceeded to "roll" all around the neighborhood. I would switch to second gear every now and then but that was about it for the first week.

Oh...wait...there was that second night where my wife decided we should ride together in the neighborhood. Yeah...I knew there was something I was supposed to be telling here. Remember, I had NEVER driven a motorcycle until I bought this one. Now, two nights later, Sallie and I are on the motorcycle fixing to take our first dual ride.

I hadn't really had enough time to even figure out how to take off but Sallie was really wanting to go for a ride so after about 30 minutes of getting used to her sitting on the back seat, we slowly maneuvered out into the street and took off in first gear. Wobbly is the word I'd use here. I am thankful there was no one else in the street in my neighborhood because I was literally all over both sides of the road. It was also about 11pm.

We stopped at the first stop sign and of course I geared down into first. Look both ways...make sure no one is coming...look both ways again because it's only the second day I've ever been on a motorcycle...look both ways again...

Sallie had to finally just force me to go. Of course, the moment I released the clutch and tried to throttle the motorcycle stalled. We lurched to a stop and laughed a bit as I restarted the motorcycle. I began to ease the clutch off again and we finally took off on our awesome first ride together.

As we approached the next stop sign, I was feeling quite good about the whole thing considering. I mean, it was only the second day and I was already riding with Sallie and in control. We stopped at the stop sign. I geared down into first and began looking both ways as usual getting ready to take off again.

As we're sitting at the stop sign and I'm fixing to take off, Sallie starts slapping my back and shrieking,
"You're in neutral Jon! You're in neutral!"

In my mind I could see the awesomeness that was me and Sallie riding together. I was taking off without a hitch and we were having a blast. In reality, my bike was in neutral and I thought it was in first gear. As I eased the clutch and rolled on the throttle, I picked my feet up like every good experienced motorcycle rider knows to do and since we were in neutral, the bike did not go forward.

Instead, since my feet were already up onto the footrests, the motorcycle fell sideways and launched me and Sallie off into the road. It was a truly righteous crash as the motorcycle fell on its side and we got small bruises and cuts on our arms, legs, and hips. Sallie had a huge bruise on her hip where she met the road with some pretty sweet force! Road rash is so awesome and all the chicks dig it...except my wife who will never forget that awesome fall.

It wasn't one of those cool crashes though. It was a dorky crash where the bike just fell over and threw us off. We happened to be in front of a house and the guy came out to see if we were alright and we really only had minor scrapes. More than anything, my pride was mostly destroyed considering I had just crashed on a motorcycle with my wife. So not cool. So not cool.

For the record, I am now a very good motorcycle rider and have not had a crash since. Thank you!

When You Gotta Go, You Gotta Go

One time I was in Florida with my wife visiting her family who lives in Orlando, FL. They have this absolutely awesome place right on the lake with perfect weather and everything. Honestly, I have no clue as to why I haven't moved there yet. Maybe after writing this book I will just pick everything up and take off. I love being there in the warm, sunny weather where the only thing dangerous is that small thing called a hurricane. Yeah, I know, it's a big thing but we have tornadoes in Oklahoma so I can deal.

Anyway, one time in Florida we all piled into the car and headed to Cape Canaveral to watch one of the space shuttle launchings. I have never seen a live launch so my anticipation was high considering I'm a complete nerd and love science and all that nerdy stuff. Apparently, tons of other people are nerds because thousands of people showed up to view the launch as well.

When you go watch a launch, you can't really drive right up to the launch bay. You actually get stopped nearly six miles away from the launch area and have to watch the launch from across the water. It's still really amazing to watch that thing take off. The flames coming from the bottom of the rockets put off a really intense color that I've never seen anywhere else due to the chemical composition of the fuel. See, told you I was nerdy.

Anyway, after the launch, traffic was absolutely ridiculous. Let me repeat: Absolutely horrendous. I'll say it again for effect.

The Traffic Was Stupid. I Hated It.

We were literally sitting completely still on the interstate. Not moving an inch. No kidding, I could literally have walked much faster. And the worst part was that there were miles and miles of cars not moving. As far as the eye could see, it was just one row of cars forever.

So, we're not moving at all, sitting still on the interstate, and I have to go. And when I mean go, I mean,

I HAVE TO GO TAKE A DUMP RIGHT NOW!

I was in a predicament. Here I was on the interstate with Sallie and her parents in the car not moving and basically about to crap in my pants. We'd been sitting in the car for nearly 30 minutes by this time and I could feel it. It was that kind of thing where it wasn't going to wait for another minute. Of course, stomach problems are common to CF peeps but what isn't common is being stuck in traffic in the middle of the Florida swamplands with no bathroom in sight for literally 50 miles.

See, in the area of Florida where they launch shuttles, there isn't much other than swampy earth. It is not ideal for a human being to go trampling through the swamp looking for an outhouse. There are alligators, spiders, snakes, and other huge monstrous creatures that my imagination makes up that live out there and I was definitely in a predicament. I am deathly afraid of spiders and bugs.

Finally, time progresses to that inevitable point in which I had to poop. It wasn't like I could continue holding it or even continue praying. It was time to poop. And I had two options: Poop in the car or poop in the swamp.

Did I mention I am DEATHLY afraid of the monsters in the swamp? I hate every crawling thing that exists and if it is in my eyesight, I freak. I do not like spiders. I do not like spiders. I do not like spiders.

AND I'M IN THE MIDDLE OF THE SWAMP!

"Excuse me." I start quietly. Considering the four of us are just sitting in the car, it's somewhat startling. "I need to use the restroom."

How polite I was. Imagine though if you can that you are on a trip with your wife visiting her parents and you want to always make good impressions and be a model husband for their daughter! And then, imagine that you are about to crap all over their brand new Lexus!

"Well, the next restroom is way off." Tom, Sallie's Dad, replies.

"Oh man." And that sums it up for sure. Oh man, I was so in trouble.

"Do we have any toilet paper or napkins?"

So, we look in the trunk where Tom just happens to have some toilet paper. Thank you Jesus! At this point, evacuation of the bowels is imminent so I snatch up the toilet paper, take a huge gulp of air and go shooting off into the swamp.

No lie, I literally ran into the swamp a good ways in flip flops and found what I thought would be foliage to shield me from all the cars lined up on the stupid interstate. Yes, see, that's the other thing. All those cars were "parked" on the interstate just like us. So, there really was no way to have privacy.

I am running at this point because I'm about to poop in my pants and I rip my pants off, pull a sort of tripod stance, and let the good times roll!

I am certain that everyone in that long line of cars saw this crazy guy go running into the swamp like a maniac and take his pants down with no care or concern about spiders, snakes, monsters, or onlookers because only one thing really mattered at that point.

When You Gotta Go, You Gotta Go!

Chapter 6
Why?

○ ○ ○ ○ ▢

Why? If you have children, you have heard this question before. But, it is different when we ask it. It's not like our children. We can just tell them that we said so, and in most realities, it works. It's satisfying to the parent to answer in this fashion. But, when we are asking why, and usually it's about something extremely serious, we don't get much in the way of answers. We are just left with the question. Why?

Why me? Why my health? Why my family? Why my work? Why my finances? Why my house?

…Why me? Why not me?

Why my children? Why not my children? Why don't I have children? Why do they have children?

…Why me? Why not me?

Why my church? Why not my church? Why that person? Why this person?

…Why me? Why not me?

Why my life? Why my plans? Why not my plans?

…Why me? Why not me?

I think we all deal with this question, and not just once in our life. It's a reoccurring question, and it never really has a good answer, especially when asked from a negative circumstance.

I was born with Cystic Fibrosis. Why me? I've had to deal with hospital visits, illness all the time, and I rarely feel "good". Why me? I have PICC lines, central lines, IV lines, and ports which all include the painful insertion methods that are barely above the level of barbaric torture. Why me? I have diabetes associated from Cystic Fibrosis. Why me? I have severe asthma, numerous bouts of pneumonia and bronchitis. Why me? I take around 20 pills a day just to eat. Why me? I take insulin shots every time I eat to battle the blood sugar problems from the diabetes I developed from having Cystic Fibrosis. Why me? I get sick easier, quicker, and frequently with greater severity. Why me?

I can't have kids. Why me?

I have missed out on many fun activities due to health reasons and multiple hospital visits that always seem to fall on holidays or vacations. Why me? I have to choose what I do based on the energy requirements of the week. Why me? I can't walk across the room without wheezing. I can't run across the street or walk a flight of stairs without dropping in oxygen levels. Why me?

I have to carry an oxygen machine and breathing nebulizers to work just to make it through a typical 8-hour work day. Why me? I do 4 breathing treatments a day which take 20 minutes each time. Then, I do 2 others that take 35 minutes each. Then I do another 2 that take 10 minutes each. Add it up and that is 170 minutes unless my math is wrong. That's just about 3 hours. I generally wake up at night and cough. I never sleep well while lying down unless I've just come out of the hospital like a freshly tuned automobile. Why me?

I have arthritis. Why me? I have memory loss from all the medications I've had pumped into my system. Why me? I've nearly died a few times from drug reactions while in the hospital. Why me? My lung functions at around 30%. Right now, it's at 31%. I feel like I'm drowning and suffer heavy breathing, wheezing, coughing, and straining just to take a breath.

...Why me? Why? Why?

Chapter 6.5
The Answer To Why

○ ○ ○ ○ □

Hear the answer. I doubt you'll like it. It's sort of what you used to hear and it was so infuriating and so not an answer. As kids we hate this answer...and it seems, as adults, we haven't grown out of this childish idea that the answer to why is another answer than what we already know.

Because God said so.

Yeah. I know. It's like all those childish, angry feelings about that answer "Because I said so" come rushing back on us and we just want to throw a tantrum on the ground, throw pillows around, punch the bed, slam the door, kick the dog...etc...and overall act totally stupid. Even after all that, it's still the answer.

Because God said so.

The rain falls on the just and the unjust. God gives mercy to whom he chooses. And who are we to question God? Like Job, how can we question the GOD who created us? He created us and he could kill us. It's his sovereign right as God to do what he sees fit. And what he sees fit is perfect, because he is perfection. We are the creation, not the creator. We submit.

We obey. We shut up. In the words of this generation...deal with it.

But that's not all there is to it. God is love also. So, this begs the question again: Why?

1 Peter 1:6-7
In all this you greatly rejoice, though now for a little while you may have had to suffer grief in all kinds of trials. These have come so that the proven genuineness of your faith—of greater worth than gold, which perishes even though refined by fire—may result in praise, glory and honor when Jesus Christ is revealed.

So that praise, glory, and honor can be gained...

...That's why.

Who better to give glory to God than a person testifying of God's greatness, power, love, and mercy who has been through fire? No one believes or counts it worth anything to hear from someone who has the "silver spoon" of a life, but from me, the one born sick but has been kept by God...that's powerful. That's glorifying to God.

When I speak of His power to keep me, to shield me, to bring me back from the brink of death, to strengthen me...that is a testimony with merit for it flows from the mouth of one who has been tried in the fire but still keeps the faith! And hopefully I've learned something from these trials. Hopefully I've learned how to represent God better, love people better, feel compassion and sympathy for people. The impurities that have been removed after melting me down into liquid and then cooling me off to be formed into a cleaner and shinier thing is so that I now shine with God's glory, honor, praise, and greatness. Instead of seeing me when you look at me, you are to see Jesus Christ. I'm a mirror, but one that displays God. And it is a mirror that began very tarnished and dirty, but has become gleaming with a bright light and finish only found inside the fire...

...That's why.

Chapter 7
Anesthetic Aesthetics

○ ○ ○ ○ □

It seems that doctors and many nurses have this idea that telling you something won't hurt is actually an okay thing. It is not okay to tell someone that what you are about to do to them won't hurt when in actuality it will hurt so much that they nearly pass out.

One such time in my life was when I found out that I would have to have a nasal sinus surgery. Sinus surgery involves removal of diseased sinus tissues and improvement of the natural drainage channels by the creation of a pathway for the infected material to drain from the sinus cavities. Basically, they suck out all the nasty sinus infection and many times also improve the sinus pathways so these infectious materials can clear out quicker and easier. In my case, I had a lot of infected junk up in there that needed to be removed.

Days before the surgery, I visited with the surgeon for a pre-operative examination. We discussed the procedure, how he would be clearing out all the infected junk and depending on the case, might actually have to make modifications to the pathways in my sinuses. I told the doctor how important it was to have a breathing treatment ready when I woke up from anesthesia. In fact, I was very concerned about this. Due to decreased lung function and oxygen saturation, waking up from anesthesia is a nightmare of spasmodic coughing that usually only subsides after doing breathing treatments. Sometimes, more than one is used in a row if I am having an extra hard time stopping the cough. As bad as the spasm cough can be after anesthesia, there is always something much more important and much more prevailing on my mind. I asked the all-important question of course which was,

"Will this surgery cause me pain?"

What followed was a blatant lie and extreme disregard for morality. The surgeon looked at me and said "Nah...you'll be in a little discomfort after the operation but will be back to normal in no time." Oh, if I had only known the depths of this surgeons depraved and evil ways!

The morning of the surgery went rather normal. We hopped in the car and drove to the surgery center where I proceeded to get into one of those stupid gowns that they always make you wear. You know the ones I'm talking about. It's that stupid gown that basically covers nothing and leaves your butt completely exposed for the whole nursing staff to snicker at. I'm pretty sure that gown was created for the very purpose of entertaining the nursing staff because I promise you it doesn't entertain me at all. It's a dumb design. The gown is a dumb design.

It's stupid, I hate it.

So, after putting on the gown from hell, they put me on the table and wheel me into the surgery room. The entire way through the center, as I take my ride, I remind them to have a breathing treatment ready in case of emergency when I wake up from anesthesia. I get confirmations and head nods indicating their compliance. In comes the anesthetist with his cocktail of drugs that are sure to put me into a peaceful coma. He shakes my hand, alleviates any fear I have that I will be unsupervised while in the coma, and a nurse starts the IV line to administer the anesthetics. Then they do that dumb game where they ask you to count down to ten. If you haven't ever had a surgery then I'll explain.

Basically, they give this powerful concoction and then ask you to count down from ten to one. Almost all patients do the exact same thing. The nurse tells the patient that they will probably be asleep before they finish counting to eight. This is amusing and somewhat of a challenge to the patient and it gets their mind off of the fear and anxiety associated with surgery. It is a good idea and typically helps.

"Start counting from ten to one for me slowly." The anesthetist tells the patient.

"Okay..." the patient typically starts a little hesitantly, "...ten...nine...eig..."

Then the patient falls into a deep coma and begins drooling heavily on themselves. This is almost universally the case for all patients. That medicine is powerful and it is fast acting, designed to put you out without controversy.

My case was a little different. The anesthetist, after having administered the powerful anesthetic cocktail, tells me to count down from ten to one. So I begin.

"Ten...nine...eight...seven..." I pause because technically I was told I wouldn't make it this far. The nurse looks at the anesthetist and says,

"Hey, he made it to seven." This invokes small smiles and snickers because they are completely confident I won't make it past six. I continue in my counting.

"...six...five...four..." Now I'm a little concerned and my blood pressure is rising because I was promised I wouldn't make it near this far. See, when things go unexpected in a surgery room, patients start to freak out and this freaking out can escalate very quickly into a full scale panic attack.

The nurse is watching me closely now and the whole room is still staring at the spectacle that is this young guy still awake after having been dosed with enough meds to drop a camel.

"...three...two...one..." I pause again. "...blast off?" I look at the anesthesiologist with my eyebrow fully raised with a very inquisitive stare. He laughs nervously and says,

"Well, you are still awake."

No kidding. You are now the proud winner of the "Captain Obvious Award" for stating the absolute most obvious thing in the world. But, what he was really thinking was: Holy crap, how in the world is that kid still awake?

He waits for a little bit, all the while using calming and soothing phrases to keep me from becoming very nervous. The surgeon then walks in and sort of does a double take that I am still awake.

"Why is the patient still awake?" The surgeon asks the staff.

"Good question." The staff answers back. It was really funny to me because I knew they were all nervous about me still being awake and now that the surgeon was in the room they were sort of in trouble for not having me prepped and ready. They inform the surgeon that for some reason they will have to use a little bit more medicine to make sure I go to sleep. Then the surgeon asks a very important question to the anesthetist,

"Did you compensate for the fact that he has Cystic Fibrosis?" See, CF people don't absorb things correctly. I typically only absorb 60%-70% of the things I should, like fats, proteins, oxygen, and other things. This is why I can eat 5000 calories per day and still lose weight. I only absorb about 60% of those calories. Yes, I typically eat about 4000 calories per day but after doing the math, I only absorb about 2400 calories. Medicines also must be given at higher doses many times to counter this absorption problem.

The anesthetist looks sort of sheepish now as he realizes what has happened. He gets more meds and doses me quite well this time. In total, I'm getting about one and a half times the normal dose of horse tranquilizer and by the time he's done pushing that in the line, I'm not even able to say the first number.

"Okay, count for me" He says to me as he pushes a life stopping amount of anesthetic.

"Um...te..." I'm out.

Fog. Haze. Distant blurry images. Ghostly forms walking back and forth. Fingers and machines probing my ears, arms, and chest. Soft, cotton ball like materials stuck to my face and nose. I hear a few of the surgery technicians talking. I am beginning to wake up.

"Man, I think I'm gonna take my girl to Bourbon Street this weekend." A tech says.

"Yeah? That sounds great. I hear they have really good crawfish etouffee." Another tech responds.

While barely awake, laying there in the recovery room, I hear them and chime in with a groggy and distorted voice,

"Yep. They have great etoufee."

Enter the spasm coughing.

Remember how I wrote a few times that I kept reminding them about the breathing problem that would almost assuredly take place after I woke up? Well, they had forgotten about having that emergency breathing treatment ready.

I began coughing so uncontrollably that I was shaking and heaving within seconds. I'm sure my oxygen saturation dropped to a ridiculous level and my heart rate shot to probably 170bpm but that is nothing compared to the pain that followed. My face "blew up" ... at least, that's what it felt like.

I had a ton of gauze packed into my nose and the coughing created a huge amount of pressure. I began bleeding like crazy and it went everywhere. The gauze was blown out and so it was like an open faucet of awesome crimson blood flowing freely onto the bed, floor, and everywhere. The techs freaked a bit and I'm sure it was due to the sight of the bleeding and spasm coughing guy in the recovery bed.

I couldn't breathe. Between the lack of oxygen, the spasm coughs, and the blood literally drowning me, I was in trouble and was desperately trying to sit up to breathe better. This was a huge mistake. No sooner had I begun to pull myself up into a sitting position than the woozy and anesthetic hang over kicked in and I toppled over the bed rail and fell on the floor. I can't imagine the sight when the techs rounded the corner with my breathing treatment to find their patient flailing on the floor in a pool of blood having the worst coughing spasm they had ever seen. I don't remember for sure but I think I threw up also. Maybe I imagined that part. Like I said, I had just fallen out of the bed dazed from anesthesia, so who really knows about that part.

They finally get me up and stabilized, get the breathing treatment going, and probably a few other things I don't remember, and I quit coughing. For a fraction of a second, I had comfort. Then, my face blew up again in pain and agony. I literally thought my face was on fire and that the fire had gone up my nostrils. It was like someone had stuck a searing hot poker straight up my nose and was just poking away at my brain. I was screaming and yelling at the staff and everyone else around me and I think I even threw things across the room. Then, they would give me some pain medication and I'd relax. It seemed though that nothing was happening or helping. My face was on constant fire and it literally was torturously painful and no matter how much I yelled and asked for help, it seemed no one was doing anything correct. I remember someone trying to give me a Darvocet which never helps. In fact, Darvocet makes me nauseous and so I kept telling them that wouldn't work. I felt each second go by due to the intense fiery pain in my nostrils and I truly thought no one was going to give me anything for the pain.

The thing that I didn't know was that I had actually been falling asleep each time they administered the pain medications but I didn't know it. So, the staff would give me some medicine, I'd go to sleep for about an hour and then wake up screaming in agony again. I guess I actually did this four or five times but it never did register as a real time difference to me because each time I woke up I still felt the same fiery pain and intense torture as if nothing had changed.

Sallie, my girlfriend at this time in our lives but who ultimately became my lovely and awesome wifey, was there also and you should hear her tell this story. It's almost funny now to hear it because I'm sure it was surreal. I would scream and freak out, get medicines that put me asleep, wake up screaming and yelling about how they weren't giving me any help, and then we'd do the whole cycle all over again. I do remember though that I kept asking for Sallie and I remember her taking my hand. Oh the magic of that hand.

I think I even said something like, "It's your hand." I won the "Captain Obvious Award" for that one.

Chapter 8
God Is In The Mix

○ ○ ○ ○ ▢

Dr. John Kramer was a well accomplished and successful doctor in charge of my care from the years of 2003 to 2009. Dr. Kramer was 81 years old and a specialist in both pediatric and adult Cystic Fibrosis care. Extremely knowledgeable and talented, giving his entire life to the service of patients with needs like my own, he passed away at age 83 and was still working as a doctor for as long as this physical life would allow.

I met Dr. Kramer at the age of 23 in November of 2003 and I owe a lot to this man and his devotion. His knowledge, hard work, and care saved my life many times. In the years he served as my doctor, I visited the hospital in Tulsa more than 30 times. Needless to say, I took up a lot of his time. In fact, at one point, after accepting me as a new patient, he told my mom that if he had known how difficult my care was going to be, he might not have accepted me! That's the truth and that's the way he was, blunt and truthful. If you were dying, he'd probably have come in and told you "Hey, you are going to die."

There was one time in the hospital that I'd like to share with you but I need to explain a typical hospital visit so that you have enough background knowledge to appreciate the imperfection.

I live in Oklahoma City which is two hours from Tulsa where my CF clinic was located. Each visit to the doctor's office would be a two hour car ride to Tulsa. Many times I'd go to the clinic and return home the same day and even make an event out of it by visiting family in Tulsa. However, on other occasions, it was much more difficult.

Those times were when I was very sick and I knew without a doubt that a hospitalization was on the way. After a clinic visit, I would typically be admitted to the St. John's Hospital which usually took at least 2 hours to get the paperwork submitted from Dr. Kramer's office. Usually we would head to a restaurant while waiting for the submission papers and have what we began calling "The Last Supper." Food in a hospital is not great, though I know they try their best. Considering a basic hospitalization lasts at least two weeks, having that one last meal was important. We would indulge in a steak or something extremely delicious in an effort to lessen the stress and anxiety of the hospital visit to come.

My mom was the main accompaniment on these trips due to my wife needing to stay home in Oklahoma City to continue working. I will not delve into the stress that this caused here at this point. Maybe later. Let's just say that being separated from your spouse for two weeks, knowing they are sick in a hospital and being unable to visit or spend time with them is difficult. I am pained in my heart at all the time that has been stolen due to this stupid illness.

Upon admittance to prison...they would begin the intravenous medications. In the beginning of my hospital career these were administered with a basic IV line, but after a few days of powerful medications running into weak veins, the IV would be changed out and moved to a vein that wasn't in fiery pain. There were times I remember the pain so severe that I couldn't sleep. I also remember the coldness of the arm. I know it sounds strange, but my arm would feel on fire at the location of the IV entry but very cold everywhere else. Kind of like disconnected, it would look at me, like it wasn't even really part of my body, desiring to be relieved of the torture that was stuck in it. Has your arm ever looked at you as if it has its own personality? Have you ever scratched an IV? It hurts. I advise against it. And there's always itching from the hole where the IV actually dives in the skin. And the tape.

Oh God the tape!

Really, sometimes the tape is worse than anything else. I hate removing tape from a hairy arm! It's stupid, I hate it!

They eventually started using longer IV lines, denoted as PICC lines and Central lines which are inserted in similar fashion which I explained in a previous chapter. So, we've got the super IV line introduced and the meds are running well without causing arm pain or "vein" pain. Vein pain. Vein pain. Say it real quick, it's funny and it rhymes. Vein pain!

I must go back in steps a bit to one of the most frustrating things in the entire world. The pre-admittance process before I actually get admitted. This is where I sit in a little bitty office coughing my head off, feeling depressed that I am about to enter this prison again for the billionth time, and having the pleasure of listening to some young girl ask me if I want to settle my medical account that is currently on file with the hospital. Do you know how much it costs to spend two weeks in the hospital on IV medications constantly? I think my cheapest visit was around $20,000 dollars. You can appreciate it more if I spell it out in real words…twenty **thousand** dollars. And the best part is they ask me…

"How would you like to take care of this?"

As if I have the money. Seriously, from the years of 2005-2008 I was unable to work. So the idea that I could "take care" of even one visit, much less the fifteen previous visits that had piled up, was insane. Yet, every time, I was sent to pre-admittance and they'd ask. So, I devised ways to answer.

"I'd love to take care of it quickly." That was a good one. Or… "With your credit card." That one didn't go over so well one time. "I'd love to just forget it…can we do that?" This one actually got a laugh. One time they asked for a hundred dollars up front. That made me laugh! Oh the comedy…

My insurance paid every time. That's the catch of all this money humor. Insurance pays loads and loads into the pockets of the hospital and its staff and doctors, well over what the medications cost of course. As an example, a 24-hour bag of TPN, Total Parenteral Nutrition, which is basically fats and weight gaining junk, costs $1500 dollars per bag. I use one a day, for two weeks, which is 14 bags. For those of us not so quick at math let me break it down easily.

$1500 dollars * 2 weeks (14 days) = $21,000 dollars.

Need a valium yet? That's just one medicine during one visit, one trip to the hospital, one "session". Do you remember how many times I said I'd been there, in that prison, among that stress, away from my wife…

…when you take the valium, make sure you drink plenty of water.

Now that I've created a great setting, I'd like to share a particular visit in January of 2009 where I went through all of what we just discussed but at this time in my life, I'd had a "port" put in. A port is a device that sits under the skin that is then accessed by a hooked needle to allow the IV meds to be infused into the body. Cancer patients have these to help them with all the powerful and toxic medications. I have one to help me with all the powerful and toxic medications required to treat Cystic Fibrosis. Mine is located on my left chest wall, just above the chest muscles, and it sticks out like an extra finger. I do not like it. I have issues with it. We won't discuss them. My wife has named it though. She calls it the "Port-O-Jon". At least it's not "Port-O-Potty". After accessing my port and hooking me up to some powerful medications, all was well....

...for about three hours.

Then, one of the most awesome experiences I've ever had took place. I have been through a lot of pain in my life. Really, that's not a joke. But I began developing a reaction to the medication in the form of coughing. It was like I had swallowed sand or more like I had inhaled sand. I felt this inflamed, irritated, and scratchy feeling in my chest and my breathing became labored to the point that I really wasn't breathing. They hooked me up to the oxygen machine to help with that and gave me some allergy medicine. It soothed the problem...

...then I got the headache.

I need to be specific here. A headache is nothing. We all get those right? I mean, we all get that headache where your vision begins to go away and blur, you can't walk straight, can't remember where you are, and begin to vomit constantly for 3 days right? We all get those.

I really thought my head was going to pop. It was like a nuclear reactor was overheating in my brain and threatening to explode out of the confines of my skull. My doctor was concerned that I was going to have an aneurism so they loaded me with morphine and then...

...nothing.

It's not that good kind of nothing that is usually associated with morphine though. It was like not taking anything. In fact, it continued to get worse. Blurry vision, confused and jumbled words, confused and jumbled thoughts, and constant pain accompanied by the ever pleasant vomiting every 15 minutes. I remember stumbling out of the bed to go throw up in the bathroom. It got so bad that even the nurses were concerned since they'd never seen anyone this bad off. And I was on the cancer floor! Seriously, I'm on the cancer floor in a hospital and the nurses are saying they've never seen anything like this? That makes a person really concerned.

It got so bad that I really thought I'd die. I've been through pain but this was an intense and specific pain in my head. At one point I remember actually telling God that He could do me a favor and just let me die. I never actually "wanted" to die, but at that point I wasn't against it either. I found myself lying in front of the toilet in a little hospital bathroom in the dark all the while puking and coughing and I felt like I was going to die. I don't really remember any other time in my life that I felt so close to dying. I had this crazy fear that my head was going to fall off and plop down into the toilet and that would be in the newspaper later in the week.

...This just in...
...Freak death involving head falling off into toilet...

I found myself in the dark. It was really dark too. Not just physically. I was crying, and in pain, and freaking out, and felt like a lizard crawling around in front of that toilet. My headache was so severe that I was sort of having one of those out of body moments. I began having a discussion in my head with myself about my dying right there in front of that toilet. I remember the conversation.

"Jon, you are dying." My mind said.
"But, I don't want my head to fall off into the toilet." I said to my mind.
"Grow up, that's not going to happen. It's going to explode instead. You really are immature."

It went on like that for about twenty or so minutes, back and forth, nothing really making sense. I remember the feelings though. I remember praying too. I remember asking God why in the world this was happening and what possible good could even come of this? What is the benefit of my suffering with this headache, with my crawling around like a lizard on the ground, and with my puking and pain? What is the point? I remember asking him that if I was going to die to let it happen sooner than later.

I remember feeling like I was in an ocean of chaos. I was tossing back and forth on the waves of destruction, headed into the mouth of death. And, I really felt alone. Everyone else in the room, or actually outside of the bathroom, was helpless. They were powerless. They were "outside" the bathroom. The lights were off due to my sensitivity to light and I was alone in a bathroom fixing to die...

"I am right here."

I remember the words. I don't know for sure if they were audible to me but they were there. God told me he was there. And that's all he said. There was no lightning, no thunder, no crashing, no earthquake, and thank God no tornado. There was just His presence and His spoken words that were so simple. And in that little bitty moment of quiet reassurance, I was okay.

Peace. It was truly peace that passes understanding. In the face of all the pain and torturous things, both physical and mental, I had spiritual peace. It does pass understanding. What I understood was that my headache was so severe that I was going to die. What I understood was pain and depression, fear and anxiety, and a certain overwhelming confusion. But what I got was peace. So, I got off the floor, hobbled to my hospital bed, laid down, and lost track of the following days.

My situation didn't change for three more days. I actually don't remember one of the days. I literally have no memory of the entire 24-hour period and while that is scary, I still have peace even now. It's a powerful peace lasting longer than just that time. It is a memory, an "altar", that reminds me of the power of a small voice that God sent to me.

No matter the situation, God is there. He is "right there", not just on your side or behind you, he's "right there" in the middle, in the center of it all. He's in the mix.

Chapter 9
Port-O-Jon

○ ○ ○ ○ ▢

I wasn't sure if I was going to write anything about this or not. I have severe psychological trauma associated with my port that I have since overcome. But, every now and then, it creeps up on me.

A port, or port-a-cath, is designed to permit repeated access to the veins through a device implanted underneath the skin. This device has a small catheter that extends into a vein, which in my case was extended in to the main aorta so medicines could be administered without having to start PICC lines or basic IV lines. A port is generally inserted in the upper chest just below the clavicle or collar bone. Since I had been having more and more visits to the hospital, I was advised that I should have a port placed so I would not have to have so many PICC lines and IV lines placed in my arms. This sounded like a good idea.

The surgery to install my first port was rather lack luster. Nothing weird happened in the surgery room but I can promise you this, the pain was enormous after surgery. For nearly a month I felt as if I had been kicked in the chest by a horse. No, actually, it was like someone had taken a sledge hammer and just slammed me in the upper chest area. I could barely move for an entire week and was never again able to really play golf. The location of the port and the way you swing a golf club just doesn't work together. After a month or so, I was able to get back to normal but I have really never been able to play golf or do bench presses. I am told there is a possibility of "popping" the line if I exert too much pressure on the chest wall. Nice...maybe you should have told me that before you inserted this thing in my body you demonic surgeon.

I remember the first time I saw my chest though once I was healed. I had this small, half dollar sized device that stuck out about an inch off my chest wall. The skin sort of pulls up and it creates a small hill on your chest. Now, I am pretty much the epitome of perfect physique and manliness, so this absurd looking "bump" on my chest wall was so completely weird looking that I truly think I suffered a small but quite real psychological episode. For about a year I would stare at my chest as if by just looking at it long and hard enough I could make it disappear. I guess I struggled with my self-image and the change that had taken place. I did not like the "bump". In fact, I hated it with a passion. I still think it looks sort of like a stubby deformation growing under my skin.

It's stupid. I hate it.

My wife though has done something rather weird. She has given it the name "Port-O-Jon." Randomly and without warning, she will sometimes poke "Port-O-Jon" for no reason. Also, she has something else she does that is just really bizarre.

Sometimes she will put her head on my shoulder, pretending to rest there as if we are having a romantic "head-on-shoulder" moment like in the movies. However, Sallie then starts to turn her head slowly and then bites my shoulder. Yes...you read that correctly. She bites me on the shoulder after pretending to rest her head. Weird I know, but weirder than that is when she bites my port. Sometimes, she'll rest her head on my shoulder but I can feel her start to slide a bit and then she literally bites my port. Yeah, I know...I have the best wifey ever!

My port had to be replaced in 2003, so I did the whole pre-op examination thingy again and of course I was told that it would not be too painful and I'd probably be back to normal activity within the week. Liars. I had by this time learned of the depths of all surgeon's depraved and evil ways! Yes...that's the exact same sentence I used in the previous chapter about the other surgeon. See...I told you surgeons were evil and monstrous. Their iniquity knows no bounds!

So we go through the same exact setup to get ready for surgery. I'll shorten it to just the following explanation. Stupid gown. More than the usual amount of anesthesia. I'm comatose. All is good cause I'm asleep and really don't even care what is taking place. In pre-op I'm told they'll make an incision in my chest, remove the old port, put the new port in place, thread the catheter to the correct line, make an x-ray of the position to make sure the line is in place, and then they'll suture me up and I'll be as good as new.

Now, if that is all there was to the story, this would be a boring and very short chapter. But, seeing as how this is a story about me, then what is supposed to happen can never be what really happens. As with all pre-op information, they forgot to include the part about what they would do when I woke up during surgery.

Yes, I actually did wake up during surgery.

It must have been somewhere around the first quarter of the surgery because they hadn't quite removed the old port from my chest wall when I literally woke up. I heard the surgeon saying something like the following,

"What is the deal with this port?" He was trying to remove the old port and it had become encased in a small pocket of skin. More information is needed for you to understand this part.

Apparently, our bodies do not like foreign objects implanted in them. For this reason, sometimes the body will create a separate "skin" or protein encasing around the foreign object.

In my case, my body hates all things foreign and had created a little pouch around the device successfully segregating it from the rest of my body. The line still worked of course but the device itself was completely contained in this separate compartment as if the device was in "time out" for being a bad foreign object.

This casing was causing trouble though for the surgeon. As I woke up, I heard him saying,

"Can you give me the pliers? This thing is completely stuck in here." I am sure he was talking about my port being stuck in the casing but I only know that after the fact. Imagine hearing that while still in surgery and not knowing what he was talking about.

I felt some pulling and tugging and heard the pliers sort of clink as they closed and opened. I remember the surgeon, possibly with the help of another technician, using all their strength trying to pull that port out of my body. I remember feeling the pull on my chest and actually felt my whole body sort of shift from their combined force. It felt weird. I think that is an understatement but luckily I did not feel any pain. It was just weird to hear the staff doing their work and talking. Then I heard another person talking.

"Do you think he can feel that?" It was sort of said I think as a joke since they knew they had to use more force than normal to get the port out. Since I was supposed to be asleep, I don't think they were concerned about comedy. That's when I actually spoke.

"Yes, I can feel that." I opened my eyes also when I said it.

It was definitely not what they were expecting. There was absolute silence for the span of eternity and then the surgeon said,

"He's awake." Ding, ding, ding...you win the award also!

"Um, he's awake...please put him back to sleep." If you can imagine the tone in which a surgeon would say that after being shocked that his patient had awoken then you can get the

whole humor of the situation. They dosed me good and proper
and I went back to sleep. No harm, no foul, but it was weird.
Needless to say the conversation with the surgeon after that
was extremely funny. He came in to see me after I recovered
from the spasm coughing like I always have after anesthesia and
asked me about a zillion questions, all regarding me waking up.
I assured I had not felt any pain and that I wasn't going to sue
them. I'm not really into the suing thing. Doctors try their best
and they are human. No one can account or plan for a patient
like me waking up during surgery.

That's just weird.

Chapter 10
When The Meninges Get Unhinged

○ ○ ○ ○ ▢

One day my new friend Matt and I decided to have lunch at The Rib Crib, a barbecue restaurant with awesome ham and turkey. Yes, that's a free plug for Rib Crib, but I seriously would accept compensation. Ahem...Rib Crib...are you reading? I'll expect the check in the mail.

We'd been planning this lunch for some time and had been having trouble connecting due to conflicting schedules. He had just moved to Oklahoma City and begun attending church with us so I was eager to get to hang with the new guy.

He picked me up and we headed out to eat, all the while talking and laughing like most people do when they are just relaxing and having fun. During the ride to the restaurant I was telling him different things about myself, different stories, and I noticed a few times I was having a lot of trouble getting the words out. But, more than trouble, I was actually saying other words than the ones I planned to say. For instance, I had been talking about how I loved music and how since he was a drummer we needed to jam together sometime. But the word for drummer came out as "elephant." Yeah, I said something like the following:

"Hey man, since you are an elephant ... er ... elephant ... er ..."
I paused here because I was slightly caught off guard at the
weirdness, "...er...man what is the word? Drummer!"

It was kind of strange, he laughed and I laughed awkwardly,
and then went on into the restaurant that we had arrived at.
We were ushered to a table, sat down and ordered, and
continued our relatively normal luncheon.

I began to slur a few things I was saying and he asked me
about it. I noticed I had developed a pretty serious headache
but thought little of it considering I live in Oklahoma City where
the allergy level is astronomically difficult to deal with. I have
all that "other stuff" too, so I just thought it was a headache.
But, the more we talked, the more my words were coming out
completely weird and jumbled. I began to say the completely
wrong words for things.

In my mind, I would think the word "drink" and instead say
"toes", or substitute a completely unintelligible word for
something else. It was like I was drunk. I started noticing my
vision blurring too. The waitress brought our food but by this
time I was having a pretty serious head ache and started getting
concerned about my inability to form the correct words. It was
like something had taken control of my brain and mouth and
was substituting the wrong things. It took nearly all of my
concentration just to eat and form complete sentences without
gibberish flying out.

Then, I knocked my drink into his lap. He was sitting across
from me and when I reached for my drink, I literally knocked it
directly into his shirt and lap. I knew something was wrong
because I wasn't even able to articulate the wording to even
apologize. I got up and realized I wasn't getting out of that
restaurant without him helping me. That's the other sign I knew
I was in trouble but I still hadn't really escalated the threat level
to red. I was still at yellow, or slightly orange.

When we arrived back home, he was really concerned. In
fact, even though he really didn't know me too well, he insisted
on coming in. I did something I rarely do and went to my

bedroom and literally laid down while my company was in my house. My headache was hurting so badly that I couldn't function. My back was literally seizing in weird muscle spasms. I was having so much trouble even just lying there. I thought maybe sleep would help and that it was just some bad allergy headache or at worst a migraine.

My wife arrived home not too shortly thereafter. Matt told her what had happened and how I was sort of acting drunk and having a headache. He told her the drink story and how we had to leave lunch due to me being sick. No doubt he was a little freaked considering this was our first time hanging out. What fun! Get a drink spilled on you and then get to watch a person slur their speech and substitute completely random words in their sentences that absolutely doesn't make any sense at all. I'm sure that he thought I was really out of it but I also think he realized I was really having something weird happening.

My wife came in, took one look at me, and called my mom. Mom showed up in what seemed like light speed since I was really not aware of anything anymore and took one look, bundled me and my wife up in the car, and sped off to the OU Medical Center emergency room. She really didn't talk much or explain what she thought the problem was but obviously it was serious enough to take me to the emergency room.

A side note. I never go to emergency rooms. Doctors find out I have Cystic Fibrosis and won't touch me. Their specialty is in generality, not something as crazy specific as CF. Also, even if they would really try, they'd fail. Normal doctors can't really handle this level of ridiculous illness. There are a million factors to think and know and only the weirdest of the bunch specialize in the ridiculous. So, for my mom to scoop me up and rush off to an emergency room was serious. It was huge.

I had sort of become a vegetable with small moans. The pain in my head was so severe I couldn't even think and if I had any thoughts, they were very freaky and weird. I felt like I was in a bowl of Jell-O. That's the best way to put it. My limbs felt rubbery and detached from my body. I was sort of out of body anyway by this time. My thoughts and mind were very distant and far off. I was in such pain that I was crying and hunched over and to this day I don't remember the car ride other than the bumps in the road. The drive to the emergency room felt like an eternity in that car and every single bump was like an explosion in my brain. I remember floating things in my vision also. Weird I know.

My back was in a repetitive spasm routine. It would seize so severely that I'd be forced to stretch out, as if my muscles wanted to detach from my skeleton. It was like someone had attached battery cables to my fingers and turned the electricity on full blast. I felt like I was in a literal electric chair causing every muscle in my back and eventually my legs to "stand out." They did too. They literally stood off my skeleton in a clenched state and it really felt as if they were going to come out of my skin.

This was a severe pain. It was so severe that I don't remember it. It's sort of like my memory was wiped of the pain. I know it was rough. I know I probably yelled and moaned and every other imaginable reaction but I honestly don't remember the severity. I even try to think about how it felt and it's hard to recall how I ever got through something so painful.

Then, I sat in the emergency room in this state for five hours. I should have probably segregated this sentence, so here it is in better, more emotional and dramatic form.

I sat in the emergency room in this
state of pain for FIVE hours.

My pastor and wife came to the emergency room and sat with us. I bet he prayed for me. In fact, I imagine him walking in, seeing this nonsense, and laying hands on me. I imagine the prayer and all that but honestly I don't remember any interaction. I only remember him coming. Trust me on this, if you are a pastor, that kind of generosity and kindness is remembered forever.

I thought I was going to die right there in that stupid ER. I really was sort of caught up somewhere else though. It's so hard to explain the way you get when you are experiencing unrelenting and unimaginable pain. Smash your head with a hammer and electrocute yourself over and over without stopping. That would get you close to experiencing the ferocity of the feelings I had during this waiting in the ER. It was never ending. Constant and to use a word previously used but can't be overused in this situation...unrelenting. I really thought I was dying. Not just going to die, but actually in the exact process of losing my life. I had the real belief that I was in the process. It wasn't just one of those "I'm gonna die" moments like before. It was real serious and I completely believed it. And it's almost impossible to explain this experience.

It's like grasping at a rope that keeps moving. You don't get upset but just continue trying to grasp this rope. At the top of this rope is something important but you know that you must grab on before you can reach the important object at the top. And that's the feeling. It never ends. You just exist in this continuous loop of trying and failing to grab the rope. It's like a computer program caught in an infinite loop. It will never finish, never end. But the weirdness of it all is that it's like a hazy dream atmosphere. It's like you leave this earth during this painful time and don't even really experience the pain personally. You literally zone out and get transported to a place that exists where few have truly swam in.

And that's another part of it. It's like being in water. You swim in this place. You float in this place. You do not have substance because you nearly don't exist. Yet, in this place, is the feeling of extreme weight and importance. There is something there, and it's your goal to locate it, but you can't and most likely won't ever find it. But it's warm. It's inviting and it's almost like you never want to truly leave, though you know you are sort of out of place by being there at all.

That's hard to understand. I know.

They finally call me in to the examination room and begin questioning me on all kinds of things. I literally had to put my entire being into concentrating on every word that came out of my mouth; otherwise, I would slur crazy nonsense. They asked me how I felt and it probably took me twenty minutes just to get one paragraph out of my mouth without it containing words that held no meaning. It was so strange. I felt like my brain had been hijacked. My thoughts were not my own and they were throwing out words and feelings that absolutely were not mine.

They moved me to the back and had me lay down. They started an IV and took some scans and such that doctors always do. They eventually decided that I might need pain medicine.

"Thank you Jesus for allowing man to create such things as Morphine and Demerol. You are infinitely awesome and loving to allow these things to exist. "

It was immediate relief. It was so good in fact that I began laughing and crying all at the same time. It was miraculous, as if God himself had come down, touched my brain, and relieved my every problem. If you have never experienced the relief that this type of pain killer can create, you are missing out. Of course, that also means you haven't been in pain which is great also. I say this respectfully that I am so very thankful for pain medications, not only here in this specific story, but all through my life when I have been plagued by the pain that is associated with terminal illness.

They sent me home with some medicines. I didn't fare well. In fact, the next day we had to pack up and travel to Tulsa to visit with my actual CF doctor. I was having the same problems of spasms and headache. I was slurring constantly and I existed in that weird place mentally. My parents and my wife were scared and so we headed on to Tulsa. It was the same horribly painful car ride but this time for a much longer bout of eternity. Once we arrived in Tulsa, they whisked me away into the examination rooms and proceeded to poke and prod at me for a while.

I am told they did a spinal tap. Now, I am also told this is extremely painful but I do not remember it at all. I remember them telling me about it and how it may hurt but the pain in my head and body was so much worse that there was really nothing that would have been its equal. They finished with the procedure and everything seemed to be normal looking and the doctor felt certain there was no problem. The spinal fluid they had extracted was clear which was a good sign indicating that I did not have any major infections. After analysis though, it was determined without a doubt that I had spinal meningitis. Yeah...I know right?! Spinal meningitis. Incredible.

Spinal Meningitis is a term for inflammation of the meninges-membranes covering the brain and spinal cord. It affects the brain and spine simultaneously. I spent two weeks in the hospital in severe muscle spasms and intense headaches due to the misfiring and inflammation. I was lucky though due to having a great doctor with compassion. He'd actually suffered through spinal meningitis himself and so knew exactly what I was going through which helped a great deal in getting those pain medications. There is no way on earth I'd have ever gotten through the illness without the pain medication.

I'm not sure what I really learned. At the time I did not know that it was such a severe sickness. I've been sick all my life so what's another problem to me, but I later found out that this disease can cause incurable secondary defects like blindness, deafness and brain damage and can even be life threatening. I've noticed that people really have a strange reaction when I tell them that I actually have had spinal meningitis before. They sort of look at me like I'm from another planet and whisper quietly among themselves.

Of course to me, it's just another example of God pulling me through something that has shaped me into what I am now. I know God was with me during this disease. He's always there.

And maybe that's the simple lesson to the whole spinal meningitis thing anyway. God is always there even when my meninges freak out.

Chapter 11
The Pessimist and The Optimist

So God had this plan all along I'm sure to pair me up with an optimist. I am naturally pessimistic and I tend to blame this on the health problems and their repercussions. See, I have never been able to just up and do whatever I want. I have to be real about the consequences of playing in the grass, walking outside when it's windy, or even just riding my motorcycle. Yes, I have a motorcycle. I know…I am awesome!

So, I met this girl when I was about sixteen years old. Right before I took off for that amazing church camp season in Louisiana, I attended a small band party. I was in band. Yes, I am a super nerd, a techie, and I work on computers. So, yes, I am the band geek. She was too. We didn't talk a lot but she did force me to play a silly game where you mimic animals with your hands and make weird noises. Anyway that was my first real memory of Sallie.

She has this amazing ability to be optimistic even when the results are obviously not going to be very good. I think this was by design. Without someone to balance my constant ability to find the negative, I'd probably never do anything. I'd probably just sit around and wait for impending doom. No, I'm not quite that bad, but I do get obsessive sometimes about the facts, which then make me only consider the negative side of those facts, the ramifications and consequences which tend to not be so positive. This is especially true of my health...like I already pointed out. I was just checking to see if you are paying attention.

Sallie grew up like many kids which consisted of a happy home life until the divorce. Ah, there's that divorce thing again. Believe me when I tell you from the experience I've had with the young people as a youth minister, and of course my own experience with my parent's divorce, it is the number one problem in our world and it jacks our kids up to no end. It is impossible to convey the emotional and mental trauma that these kids go through and it's all due to the selfish sins of their parents.

As a side note, if you are a father or mother planning to divorce, you need to see through the lies the devil tells you. You aren't the only one who will be affected. You aren't the only one who will have a lifestyle change. While you are out committing adultery and having a grand old time in your sin and debauchery, make sure to remember that your kids are going to suffer an emotional explosion of pain, suffering, and agony of which you have no ability to understand. They will always remember and it will always haunt your relationship with them. Your selfishness and inability to live for God is what they will remember about you most. They will also believe that you do not love them or want them and will seek that love somewhere else. As my Pastor says regularly in his sermons, "Remember, you are not the only one taking the trip."

Back to Sallie. After the divorce of her parents, things got really screwed up. After a few years, her Dad had moved to Florida which put a huge amount of space between them for the first time. Sallie's mom then met a man in a bar who she got married to rather quickly after about two months and so Sallie and her brother were moved into his home. After about a year, the step-father kicked her brother out and he ended up moving to Florida and reuniting with his father. This left Sallie living in a new environment with an alcoholic step-father.

Anytime the words "alcoholic step-father" come into play, it is most likely to be viewed with pessimism. Sallie was nine years old at the time of divorce and twelve years old at the time her mother remarried and moved in with the "alcoholic step-father."

Sallie hasn't told me many stories about this time in her life. I think it is because there aren't many good stories to tell of this time period in her life from age 12-17. I know from the stories she has told me that she felt alone and very scared of her step-father. He was always drunk and always inappropriate. Being the time when most girls are branching out into the realm of boys, entertainment, and friends, stories of fear, intimidation, and abuse aren't the ones you want to remember and cherish. But, this was her reality.

Instead of getting to chase boys or getting chased by boys at school, she was chased by a perverted step-father. Instead of being innocent and fun loving, she was tormented and fearful of every moment in his presence. She took every opportunity to not go home by sleeping over at friends' houses and spending every possible moment somewhere else. She used to get physically ill and shake uncontrollably when she had to go home due to the unforeseen and often inappropriate actions made towards her by her step-father. The only things in the refrigerator at home were beer and more beer. There was rarely food and or cooked dinners. Without the charity of friends, Sallie would have gone without food most nights.

Rick was his name. He had strange rules for his home and in my few times dealing with him he reminded me of the type of man that ruled his women with fear and intimidation. I know that is not a politically correct way of writing but that is the way he was and the best way to describe his character. He was that guy that dominated women and tried to constantly be the alpha male. There was no safety, security, normalcy, or love in his presence. There was only perversion, abuse, and neglect from a sexual predator.

One such event was when Sallie was 12. Like most young girls, she wanted to get a belly button ring because her friends were all doing it. Being a typical girl, Sallie had planned to just go to a regular piercing studio to get this done but instead her step-father took it upon himself to persuade her into letting him give her the piercing. Since she feared his anger, she agreed to let him try. He proceeded to hold her down on the kitchen table while he used a nail to pierce her belly button. Of course it got infected and the pain was extremely intense but her fear of that memory is what lasted.

Somehow she came out with dread and terror of this memory. I have heard of people doing piercings this way and possibly having success but the left over ramifications of this event left Sallie extremely traumatized and fearful of Rick. Sallie lived in this weird atmosphere constantly and never really knew what to expect. The mental fear was overwhelming and she lived with it at all times.

When was the next attack? When was the next sexual advance? For her 13th birthday, Rick bought her a skimpy lingerie teddy and tried to persuade her to model it for him. Most girls that endure that kind of mental abuse end up with terrible self-images and end up carrying out acts that have severe life altering consequences such as prostitution, drug use, alcohol use, and suicide. He constantly made sexual advances and many times blatantly offered sexual advice about how she should be with other boys.

When a young girl is treated as a sexual object of lust and desire it is shattering to that young girl forever. The fact that it was continual gave Sallie the "no way out" feeling. This is when young people feel there is no way out of their situation and this leads many to suicide. I fear for their eternal life and the consequences that will follow anyone who carries out physical and mental abuse against children.

We used to go to Sonic all the time and just talk for hours. Cheese fries for her and cheddar bites for me. We'd sit and just spill our problems and emotions out about our families. My family was falling apart due to adultery and at that time my Mom was sort of a zombie. I'm pretty sure my Mom was dealing with similar feelings of abandonment and rejection after having been married for twenty years to my father. I spilled my feelings out about CF and being sick all the time and the struggles that existed. Sallie's daily life was also a struggle for survival against a real threat in the form of an abusive step-father. She never knew from one day to the next what form of abuse she'd encounter.

We used each other and leaned on each other for support, love, care, and friendship. I needed someone I could trust and confide in about all the things that were in my thoughts and most of my friends had never had any life experiences to even remotely be able to understand me. She needed someone to care about her and listen to her. I know now that God put us together at a time when both of us could easily have slipped off the radar and made horrible mistakes as teenagers.

But God...

She has been through almost every single hospital session I've ever had. Remember, we met at the age of sixteen, and that's when I started the visits to the "prison". She has been by me through PICC lines, Central Lines, and nasal surgeries. She has been by me through near death reactions to medications, allergy reactions, and every other reaction. She has also seen my worst times, my dark times, and my horrible rebellious times. She has cleaned up my puke.

One time I was finishing up a breathing treatment and had taken an Ambien to help me sleep. Sometimes the medicines are a stimulant which makes sleeping very tough, so to combat that, we take other meds that make us sleepy. Well, for whatever reason, this one made me nauseous as well. I began burning up and sweating like crazy, and of course, since it was a sleep aide, I was woozy and sleepy. Sort of like being drunk and unable to really control motor functions completely.

I literally stumbled into the bedroom, tore off all my clothes, and then proceeded to bounce off the walls as I nearly fell into the bathroom. I then proceeded to puke all over the toilet and the walls in a hazy stupor. It wasn't the normal vomit either. It was extreme projectile and it was AWESOME!

Then, for whatever reason that I absolutely can't remember, I got in the shower to wash off. I vaguely remember any of this due to the "Ambien amnesia" but after the shower I ran to the toilet again to throw up and just stood there. By this time my wife is awake and she comes into the bathroom to find puke everywhere on the toilet and her naked husband basically holding onto the wall to maintain balance. She grabs some towels, begins to start cleaning all the puke, looks up, and there in her face is my bare butt as I stand sort of spread out over the toilet waiting to puke again. She tells it much better and with much more comedy. In fact, it's her favorite story to tell.

Sallie has been there through lack of money also. We got married in 2004 and in 2005 I retired. Well, it was more like forced retirement due to terrible health. I was in the hospital nearly ten times a year and couldn't keep my job although I had been blessed with lenient and understanding bosses. So, I retired at age 25. Right after that, Sallie was fired from her job.

Let me rewrite that so you catch it. Sallie was fired from her job after I retired. At age 25, retirement isn't where you receive that large 401K you've been building. At age 25, the 401K is more like 40 bucks.

Insert stress here.
Insert panic here.
Insert anxiety here.
Insert depression, fear, and overall freaking out here.
Insert "What are we going to do?" right here.
Insert "Is my wife going to stay with me through all this?"

Here I was at age 25 and unable to work and provide for my wife. Here I was at 25 and without health to even take walks, expend energy, or even breathe well. Forget spending time at the park. I'm allergic to it all and don't have the oxygen saturation to even begin strenuous activity. A man is supposed to be able to be a man and be energetic and athletic and all that stuff and I could barely walk across the room without wheezing and heaving. It affected every aspect of our life together and the lack of health coupled with the loss of jobs was nearly overwhelming. I felt like a failure as a husband. I felt like a failure overall and wondered sometimes about the likelihood of our marriage lasting under such pressures and stresses. What woman is going to endure this type of life? What woman is going to endure constant struggle, constant fear, anxiety, and stress?

God doesn't make mistakes. What God has put together is not a mistake. What God does is not a mistake. God doesn't make mistakes. God takes imperfection and creates perfection.

Sallie had endured stress before. Sallie had been victorious over anxiety and fear before. She didn't leave me. She persevered and got hired on at a temp job in an oil company for $10 dollars an hour. Medical bills piled up. Bills in general piled up. Basic necessities became very difficult to pay for but we never went without. Our church made a food donation to us one time. My Mom and step-Dad helped us all the time. My Dad helped, my Grandparents helped, and even my uncles, especially my Uncle Lyle, sent us money many times and they have never really had much money ever. I am appreciative and humbled that they cared enough to help us. I am in your debt and hope you know how thankful we really are for those times.

Most women would leave a man who doesn't have money. Most women would leave a man who was sick and couldn't provide and was unable to work and was in the hospital all the time. Most women wouldn't continue in a marriage that was that difficult, and that was all in our first two years. But Sallie is not most women.

And God doesn't make mistakes. Ever.

Sallie is definitely not most women. I guess that is why she prevailed in the presence of evil. Weighed down with every kind of darkness she remained optimistic. She went to church, went to school, fought the pressures and struggles, and succeeded in life. She finished school, succeeded in a career, and married a man who values her not for her skin but for her true worth. She balances my "realism" and tendency towards being negative. She helps me to stay healthy and have a positive mindset towards things that regularly are troublesome.
She is the perfect complement that only God could have created. She is the only truly awesome person I know and her amazing talents and abilities are so vast and truly inspiring that words fail. My life is worth something because of her and I will spend the rest of my life trying to bless her as she has blessed me. I love her as Christ loved the church...

...And she is smokin' hot!

Chapter 11.9
Aftermath

Sallie's family life has turned out much like mine has after the storms. She has a relationship with her mother that beforehand was never possible. With Rick in the picture, there was no happiness, no love, and no way out. Eventually, Sallie's mom left that disgusting man and settled with Sallie in an apartment for some time until Sallie moved out for college. Her mom showed strength in leaving an abusive man who she also feared might retaliate at her leaving.

I don't know why some men are the way they are but he was a strange one. I know God had a hand in that separation and I saw only great and wonderful things transpire because of it. Sallie and her mother have a better relationship now and her mother has thrived by having friends and family that offer hope, love, and care instead of fear, intimidation, and abuse. She actually lives a mile from us and is a very special part of our lives.

Sallie's relationship with her father also grew over the years. They share a love for Disney World since he lives in Orlando, Florida. She visits him yearly, sometimes twice a year, and they, like my dad and I, have a great relationship.

It's really amazing how God can take things that are really rough and terrible and make something great. The time I spend with Sallie and her family always reminds me that God is so powerful and is able to overcome any obstacle. Again, I don't understand God's plan all the time, but I cherish the results.

Chapter 12
Cantaloupe Knee And Friends

When I was 14 years old I attended Junior High Youth Camp in Oklahoma. Being 14 meant that I and my friends were "the older kids" on the campus with all the rights and privileges associated with being the older kids. Normally Junior Camp was held for the age group of 11-14 years of age and this was my last year that I would attend the Junior Camp since I would be too old next year. So, it was my "senior" year and my friends and I had made plans all year to make this the best youth camp we had ever attended.

After getting my sleeping bag, clothing, and everything else situated in our dorm rooms, we headed out to the basketball court. Everything took place at the basketball court including girl watching, chasing, flirting, and even some basketball playing. All the cool kids hung out at the basketball court. I have mentioned this in an earlier chapter but I was lucky to be healthy enough to go outside and play sports. I know many CF kids who probably were not, or are not, that healthy. I am thankful for the time I have been able to be active and pray that those of us who can't be active yet will be one day.

Typically we'd stay up most of the night causing havoc and getting in trouble from the dorm deans. We did the normal boy stuff like talk about girls, throw starburst candies across the room in the dark. One funny prank is to lick a starburst and then throw it across the dorm room in the dark. You hear this slap which is the starburst hitting the face of some other kid. Then, you always hear a yell or scream which is so hysterical. Yeah, kids are mean.

Anyway, camp was going well for about the first two days. It usually lasted Monday through Friday and on Tuesday I was headed to the lunch hall to eat. I was accompanied by two very pretty girls and we were laughing and talking and doing the whole flirting thing. Anyway, we went through the line and I had gotten some chicken nuggets with barbecue sauce. We headed outside to eat, all the while laughing and having fun. Now, I was talking with these two girls and of course trying to be cool and suave. It had been going pretty good for a while until the wind picked up and literally carried my plate of barbecue sauce directly into the shirt of one of the girls. The sauce went everywhere on that shirt and seriously was the funniest thing I'd seen but was definitely not cool for the girl, which meant it was really not cool for me. I of course did the whole apologizing and being concerned thing but honestly it was hilarious that my barbecue sauce had flown all over this girl's shirt. Just wanted to throw that story in for fun.

Wednesday rolled around and I started noticing my joints hurting a bit but of course I thought it was due to all the fun I was having playing basketball and staying up late in the dorms. I ignored the problem and went on my way. Wednesday night rolled around and I started having trouble walking and noticed my knees had sort of swelled a little. Of course, I ignored it.

Thursday morning rolled around and my elbows were the size of oranges and my knees had swollen to the size of grape fruits. I could barely walk to the classes for the day sessions of camp but since I was young and wanted to have fun with my friends, I kept on trying to ignore the problem. It was harder to ignore though because there was quite a bit of pain when walking and moving any part of my body. In fact, my whole body hurt and was sort of swollen. By Thursday night, my knees looked like cantaloupes and hurt so bad I could barely move.

My parents came out to camp that night to check on me. I came hobbling down the sidewalk headed up to the church tabernacle and my Mom literally freaked.

"What's wrong with you?" She knew by the way I was hobbling that there was obviously something going on that I had obviously neglected for too long.

"Nothing really. My knees seem to hurt when walking." Understatement of the year.

She made me roll my pants up and I think she about fainted out on the dirt from the sight of my huge knees. She took me home immediately and had me keep my legs propped up all night. We went to the doctor's office the next day to get some answers.

The part of this story I haven't told you is that before I went to camp I had begun taking a medicine called Floxin. Floxin has some strange side effects, one of which is swelling of joints. Well, my Mom suspected this was the case but to be sure, we visited the doctor and within about 5 seconds the doctor confirmed that I was indeed having a serious side effect to the medications.

The far reaching effects of the swelling still haunt me now. Underneath the knee cap is a cartilage that keeps the knee cap from rubbing against the rest of the knee joint. This cartilage is a thin elastic tissue that protects the bone and ensures good knee movement. I do not have this cartilage anymore because it eroded away back when I was 14 and taking Floxin. Now my knees pop and creak and I have severe arthritis making it extremely difficult sometimes to just walk around. I also have loss of cartilage in my elbows and pretty much anywhere else cartilage is supposed to exist. Needless to say, I have some serious throbbing that takes place in my joints at different times, usually when it is wet out or cold. There really is nothing like cantaloupe knee.

I'm always impressed with people who have a good memory. I do not. I tell the youth in our youth group, especially new visitors, that I ruined my memory doing drugs. It's not a lie and it always gets some strange looks from the new ones.

The medicines I have taken and the doses at which I have taken them have severe side effects. Some of these side effects are like I previously wrote about causing headaches, nausea, blurry or unfocused vision, itchy or irritated respirations, and other things. Other side effects are memory loss and hearing loss.

I noticed my memory loss a few years back around the age of 27. I wasn't working at the time and was in the hospital about 9 times that year alone and so the medicine use was nearly nonstop. I began having a lot of trouble with remembering anything people told me. No matter how hard I tried and no matter how important the information was, I nearly always forgot it. I still do this.

Just last week we had a young girl visiting our youth group. Right before church started I went and introduced myself and got her name. I told her how great it was to have her there visiting and that she was welcome to join our youth group service that night. When we all got settled into the youth service, I noticed we had a young girl visiting. I sort of motioned to her and opened the service with,

"Welcome to our youth service. I want to say what a pleasure it is to have … uh…."

Yeah, I forgot the girls name completely. And I had just met her not ten minutes earlier. I do this all the time though. So, now when I meet someone, I tell them that the odds are high I will not remember them or their name. I'm sure one day I'll find myself walking out in a field not knowing where or who I am. Oh well...such is life I guess. But, though I jest, it is a real fear of mine.

I have an incredible wife and if I forget her I will have forgotten something very precious and very priceless. I pray daily that God will not force me to suffer that kind of thing. Of course, if he does, I guess I won't really know.

I started suffering from hearing loss much earlier. I was about 21 years old when I started that mess. I used to be able to hear people's watches ticking in class but now I can't hear anything very well. One such conversation between my wife and I went as follows:

"I love DVR." My wife said. We had just gotten a DVR machine to record shows and it was really neat being able to watch TV when we had the time. We've never had much time for it, so now, when we actually do have some time, we don't have to watch those stupid commercials. Commercials are so stupid. I hate them.

"I love you too babe." I reply with all the love and care I can muster so she knows I am serious. I hear her snickering on the verge of a complete laughing fit.

"What's so funny?" I ask.

"What do you think I said?" She asks, now in tears from laughing.

"I don't know...what did you say?" I have figured it out now that I obviously didn't hear her.

"I said...I love DVR. But, I love you too Jonky." She hee-hawed after that.

Jonky is my nickname. Her nickname is Salliemander. But I usually just refer to her as wifey. And she loves to laugh, especially when I've done something goofy or funny. We both busted out laughing for hours on this one. I even still occasionally will look at her and say..."I love DVR."

My wife nearly always pulls my IV lines out. Whether it is a port line, a PICC line, or a basic IV line, she never fails to get her arms or body tangled in my IV lines and almost pulls them right out. We typically make a note of it because she always does it at least once an IV session. She's gotten better over the years of not walking across my lines. See, the lines are sometimes longer than you'd expect, and after weeks of IV lines and medicines, you tend to forget that you are even doing them. That is about the time Sallie likes to try to kill me by running into the lines and nearly pulling them out of my skin.

My dog does this also. She sometimes gets all tangled on the floor and then tries to run off. This pulls the line, nearly popping it out of my skin. So far, it hasn't been jerked out but we've come close. Even my Mom has done it a few times. I have to remind her while she is nearly having a nervous breakdown that it's okay and I'm fine and that my wife does it all the time.

One time we gave our cat an IV. It was weird because the water bulged up in a ball on her side like a tumor and then slowly fell to her stomach area. It was strange and really the only time I've ever given an IV on someone or something else. Not sure why I wrote that about the cat.

I have the smelliest fart you will ever smell. I promise. I will always win the fart contests. When I was younger, as is the case with gross boys, we'd hold contests. Of course, there were rules, but no matter what we did, I always won. Eventually, I'd just fart, even if there was no competition, and we'd all start yelling that I won. Boys are weird and gross.

We would get in a small enclosed room and then fart. The other boys would judge the fart. I remember once we held a fart contest at church. We all went into the bathroom and proceeded to fart. Most farts were pretty good with the best being around 9 out of ten. Then, it was my turn.

Honestly, it was nuclear. On a scale of 1 to 10, I probably scored around 23. No kidding, I farted and the whole group nearly puked and ran out of the room. Even after a few hours, it still stunk so bad that people would just turn right around and forget they had to use the bathroom at all. That's awesome...I don't care who you are.

One time I farted and locked the windows in the car while riding with Sallie. That was fun. Another time, I farted in the band room. Yes, I was a band nerd. I am also a computer geek. See, I am a super geek for sure.

We were in jazz band and I played trumpet. During practice one day I let out a small, ever so significant fart. It took an extremely long time to permeate the room and it sort of went in waves up through the jazz band group. As it gravitated forwards, the back row literally stopped playing and ran out of the room. The director was a little shocked and as he was about to gripe out the back row, the fart found its way to the second row where they too followed suit and ran out, leaving just the front row and the director. He was stymied and growing extremely angry. As he was just about to launch an all-out tirade against the students, he smelled the infamous fumes and literally dropped his baton and grabbed his nose. The entire room had cleared out and jazz band practice was over.

I know...I'm awesome!

CF causes strange things. Gaseous build up from the lack of absorbing fats in the intestine yield some high impact stank! Yes, that's "stank." Read it correctly and you'll get the point. It causes all kinds of problems.

I remember being on a date once and having so much gaseous discomfort that I literally was sweating from trying not to pass the gas. I knew if I actually did pass gas, I'd kill the girl I was on a date with and everyone else in the Steak & Ale restaurant. Yes, I remember where I was. I probably went to the bathroom ten times that night. She was a sweetheart though and never even said anything about how weird it was that night.

I cough all the time and this can cause some reactions among people that are germaphobes. I was watching a movie once in the theater that just came out recently titled "Contagion" which of course is a movie about a pandemic that breaks out and kills everyone. It starts out with people coughing in the movie, which I am already doing in real life, and I'm sure people in the audience thought I was sick. It is probably weird to watch a movie about people coughing and hearing a person coughing like I do. It adds a real component. It makes me laugh though and Sallie and I just loved every minute of it.

My friends are used to it though now. There are many times we'll be in the middle of a table of friends and I'll start coughing. Not normal coughing but serious spasm coughing and nearly be on the floor but of course my friends aren't even paying me attention as they rattle on in their conversation. It's nice to know I am so loved and cared for.

I have been lucky though to have a life like I have. Most people understand and after a bit of education about CF they generally have no fears of me. There are some though that are unable to overcome their phobia and I usually haven't continued friendships with people like that.

Cystic Fibrosis is a genetic disease which is not contagious considering you have to be born with it in your genes. I cough a lot. I get sick a lot. I lose weight a lot. I can't breathe ever and I have terrible digestion. It's just me. It's just my life. I have a wife, family, and great friends who have all learned to deal with this stress and who all help me deal with this stress. I am eternally grateful for all of them.

Chapter 12.9
Quality Of Life

○ ○ ○ ○ ☐

As I previously wrote, I "retired" at the age of 25 until I was 28. During those years, I was in the hospital approximately 8-9 times per year and it was one of the most difficult times I have ever faced. Being home every single day without enough energy to even walk around was devastating. During that time, I would find myself sitting in the recliner, staring at the blank television, doing absolutely nothing. One time my wife came home from work and found me just sort of zoned out. She woke me out of my zombie state and we determined I had been sitting there in that nothingness for probably three hours.

I didn't handle retirement well. I actually published a music CD during this time of Christian music that I wrote and performed but I was not built to stay home.

In 2008, I miraculously got better. There really is no other way to explain it other than God must have decided I needed to get better. I went from having 9 hospitalizations a year to having 2 and having better health and pulmonary function testing. Pulmonary Function Tests, or PFT, is a way to measure the efficiency of the lungs in terms of respiration, inhalation, exhalation, and total air volume. Most people score a PFT level of around 90% but I continually was scoring around 40%. In 2008, I began feeling better and attended a programming class in order to break into a field of work that I could physically handle. I began working downtown in OKC as a web developer in May of 2008 and have been working there for the past three years.

My wife and I began working with our local youth ministry in the church and after a few years I found myself as the youth pastor. This was not something I could have done in the dilapidated state I existed in a few years earlier. God obviously had something in mind by helping me to become healthier and I truly believe that being part of the youth ministry was a significant part of me getting miraculously better.

I wanted to work. I have always wanted to work and provide for myself. Independence is a big thing to me and I do not like to depend on others so not working was a huge problem for me. I am happy to be working but of course it provides daily challenges. I'll continue working until I can't. Unfortunately, short of a miracle that heals me completely that only God can provide, I'll have to stop eventually but I'll choose to work until then. I have a huge sushi addiction that I have to pay for!

I am currently on the transplant list awaiting a double lung transplant. Even in the time it has taken to just edit and write this book things have changed. In 2011, during the month of November, I began coughing up large amounts of blood and had to be quickly admitted to the hospital. Just in this year alone I have been to the hospital three times within the past five months. It was during this last visit that it was determined without controversy that I was to be designated as a patient in transplant status. My PFT dropped to 24% and has only risen to about 30% after that hospital session. I am told that within the next year my transplant will most likely take place.

From the looks of things, it is not going well but small miracles are still taking place that remind me that God has a plan even if I don't like all the intricacies. My work has allowed me to work from home most of the work week. This means I don't have to quit and retire again. In an economy as difficult as ours with people losing jobs all the time and unable to find work, this is a huge miracle. Having a work environment such as the one I have is so rare and amazing that I know without a doubt that God has his hand in it. I don't know what the future holds for me but I know that I am thankful to be working and productive in a career that I can actually physically handle. I know this is all possible though because of God and his weird ways of making things work that seem like they will absolutely fail.

Chapter 13
Introducing Cystic Fibrosis

○ ○ ○ ○ ▢

You probably think this should have come first but I warned you that this book didn't always make sense and how I would do weird things. See...I told you so.

There are approximately 30,000 people living with Cystic Fibrosis in the United States. The major cause of illness and death among Cystic Fibrosis people is progressive lung disease. Cystic Fibrosis is characterized by abnormal transportation of chloride and sodium across the epithelium leading to thick, viscous secretions in the lungs, pancreas, liver, intestines, and the reproductive tract.

Difficulty breathing and poor digestion are the most serious symptoms associated with CF. Frequent lung infections are treated with but not cured by antibiotics and other oral medications. A multitude of systemic problems arise such as sinus infections, poor growth and absorption rates, frequent abdominal pain and intestinal problems, poor digestion and growth, and infertility. CF attacks the entire body, leaving nothing free from the devastating and life-smothering assault that is so common with this terminal illness. Ultimately, lung transplantation is often necessary in the lives of most CF people.

Cystic Fibrosis is most common among Caucasians. At least one allele for CF is found in 1 out of 25 people having European descent. For this reason, if you are attempting to become pregnant and start a family, please have yourself and your spouse screened for this gene. You are running the risk of giving birth to a baby that may be diagnosed with Cystic Fibrosis.

The hallmark symptom of CF is salty tasting skin. This is why my dog loves to lick me nonstop. I am super tasty and she loves the salt. When I sweat, you can literally see the salt formation on my forehead and arms. This salt is the reason for my poor growth, poor weight gain, sticky and thick mucus, frequent chest infections, shortness of breath, and coughing. I am in constant danger of lung diseases as the mucus in my chest is so thick and gets infected because my body can't naturally clear itself.

I do pulmonary chest therapy daily to try to battle this problem. I have a machine called The Vest which is literally a vest that I wear. The vest is attached to an air compressor that then inflates around me, squeezing me tightly like a water life vest. The air is then pumped quickly through the vest creating a rhythmic percussive motion that beats against my chest and back. This dislodges the mucus in my lungs so I can actively cough it out. Without therapy of this nature, the mucus remains seated in my lungs harboring infections. Though not a cure, it is a definite necessity to stave off the ravaging effects of constant lung infections.

Breathing treatments open the airways. Pulmozyme, an inhaled medication, breaks the mucus down at the cellular level, creating thinner and more easily transported mucus when I cough. TOBI, an inhaled antibiotic, battles against the infections. Cayston, a new medication, also battles the infections and holds promising results for many CF people who use it.

I have diabetes also. I take insulin shots every time I eat. One time I was having low blood sugar and so I drank a lot of orange juice. Then I drank two Ensures which are weight gaining shakes. Then, after about 20 minutes, I puked all of it up. In fact, the puking was so awesome that I remember thinking I wished I had videotaped it so I could put it on YouTube. I would have been an instant celebrity! I Googled "milk and orange juice" and found out that it is not something you want to drink in large quantities because it will make you seriously vomit. I also found out it is a concoction they use in the movies to make people vomit on demand. Really? Wish I'd have known that earlier. Still, it was an awesome puke!

A lot of people have trouble wrapping their head around Cystic Fibrosis. Since it is an illness that is on the inside of the body, much of the time I never look any different than anyone else. I have had friends that I grew up with in school who never knew about me having Cystic Fibrosis. They just knew I missed a lot of school. Generally this causes confusion because as human beings not educated in a life of illnesses, we sort of expect sick people to "look sick." So when I show up at church on a Wednesday night and play the organ during service and then get admitted to the hospital the very next morning, it is quite confusing. I often hear how great I look at times that I feel my worst. My life is a daily struggle to just get by sometimes. I never really know how I am going to be doing health wise from day to day. One day I can be out riding my motorcycle with my wife and having a perfect day and the next day I can be so violently sick that I have to be admitted into the hospital for an IV session. That's life with Cystic Fibrosis and it's confusing, difficult to plan for, and always interrupts at the worst possible moments.

There's so much to say about Cystic Fibrosis. Honestly though, it's just my life. Again, I am so thankful my life is the way it is. I have a great life but I will admit, it is definitely not the easiest life to live. Not sure why I was chosen. Maybe I'll find out one day. Till then, "I love DVR".

Chapter 14
These Lungs Will Praise The Lord

There has been a good amount of time that has passed between the last chapter and this one. I had planned to publish this book in February of 2012 but ended up getting too sick to finish and so put it on hold. I began writing this chapter in September 2012, nearly 10 months after that last chapter that you just read. Much of this was told to me by my wife and mom and so it is possible that I may not get everything precisely correct but I'm sure you'll get the gist.

Chapter 14.1
These Lungs Will Praise The Lord

The Beginning Of The End

○ ○ ○ ○ ▢

As stated, I planned on publishing my book in February but didn't get to. Instead, I ended up in the hospital for nearly three weeks with a Pulmonary Function of around 28%. I endured this stay as with other stays but this one was different in that my breathing never really got any better. During my visit, I was instructed to start using a bi-pap machine which is a machine that forces air into the lungs when you inhale. It also keeps pressure when you exhale to keep your lungs open and expanded. This is all to help oxygen get to the lungs in a more efficient manner since I had gotten so weak. Left to my own energy and muscle ability, I was losing the battle to breathe. I had dropped to around 120 pounds and my color had turned a very sick, pale white. I was also losing muscle mass due to being so malnourished. Basically, the effort to breathe was killing me. So, the bi-pap became a regular part of my face.

A Bi-Pap consists of a small machine that has a tube that delivers oxygen forcefully to the patient. You wear a mask or nose mask, called nasal pillows, that is fitted to your face so air can't escape. It's uncomfortable and took a long time to get used to but works very well. While wearing the bi-pap, I was able to get some comfort. But, sleeping was nearly impossible at first. Try attaching a vacuum to your face and see how you like it. I nearly drove my wife crazy considering she wasn't getting much sleep either as I tossed and turned and fought with the hose attached to my face all night long. The nasal pillows made me look like an elephant also and I got in a habit of regularly making the elephant trumpet sounds. Whatever makes it bearable.

The months of February, March, and April were really horrendous. I didn't leave the house. I didn't attend church. I didn't go out with Sallie. I didn't work. I didn't walk. I didn't move. I didn't get to do any of the things that we all take for granted.

The reason was because I couldn't take the bi-pap machine off my face. Even at the house, when going to the bathroom, my breathing was so terrible that I would have to run to the bathroom and pray that I didn't take too long or I'd get light headed and feel like I was going to pass out. I'd start breathing extremely fast and start coughing within minutes of taking the bi-pap off. Even trying the oxygen tanks would fail simply because my body was not able to pull in the oxygen required for any type of exertion. Showers were tough because the air was heavy and moist and so I'd have to take the fastest shower humanly possible, even though I didn't have any energy, and then literally run to the couch where the bi-pap machine sat. I love showers and generally take a shower that is way too long for any one human being so this inability to relax while showering greatly frustrated me.

My routine was to get up in the morning, unplug the bi-pap from the bedroom, run it into the living room, plug it up hurriedly, put it on, and then sit in the recliner heaving from the exertion it took to just move from one room to the next.

In those three months, I didn't go to work at all. I had recently begun working from home half the week but now I was at a point where I couldn't go into the office at all because I couldn't go for ten minutes without my bi-pap and oxygen machines. Oh, I had tried to get to work with just the oxygen machines but that didn't work anymore. I'd be heaving and coughing before I even got fully dressed. If you want to see something crazy, watch me try to get dressed for work while sweating and coughing. By the time the clothes are on, they are wet with sweat, my hair is soaked, and I am on the verge of smashing everything in my house out of anger. Then, I strip it all off and reattach the bi-pap so I can get enough oxygen to slow down and relax, all the while toweling off as if I've just taken a "sweat" shower.

Now that's stupid. And I really hate it.

Fear and frustration reigned on me with thoughts of getting fired from work or let go due to illness. Thoughts of being without enough money and necessities were again on my mind like the last time I had to quit working. Of course, I was still working from home the entire week and not required to physically be at the office. I had even been reassured by my managers that the situation was just fine but you know how it is. Will they really put up with all this for just one employee who seems to be needy all the time? And how long with the grace last?

For that kind of generosity I am forever thankful to my coworkers. What a miracle it is! They allowed me to work from home every day without question. But, even in that, I was depressed at having such a drastic change of life. I was now living as if I was just waiting around to die. Not able to truly live, I was just barely surviving. Earlier I wrote about quality of life but in those three months, there was very little quality. It was more like: Just survive.

In those three months, I didn't go to church. I didn't get to participate in music or youth. Until this time, I had been the youth pastor for the past four years and it was what I felt I was placed here to do. I felt it was the job I was supposed to be doing in that local church and every day I prayed for healing so that I could fulfill that calling, so that I could get back to being with that youth group. I wanted to be the youth pastor of that awesome group of young people, watch them continue to grow in God, and have awesome fellowship together. I prayed to be able to go and play music and participate in worship and have fellowship with the church family because I knew I was supposed to be there and be part of all of the awesome and miraculous things that take place.

I didn't get to worship with the church family during those awesome services that I'd read about on Facebook or Twitter. I didn't get to see those young people get baptized, teach bible studies, or do any church work because all I could do was sit and try to breathe. And it was "try to breathe" instead of "breathe" because it was so difficult. Most of the time, the bi-pap barely kept up with me and my oxygen tanks were set at the highest levels we could safely use in the home. I missed out on a lot of what I consider life in those three months. But mostly, I missed my life with Sallie.

Sallie and I love activity but for the past few years I have been too sick to really be considered highly active. But, we never stop moving, never stop going, never stop having fun, and never stop living. We have a favorite sushi restaurant and love doing a dinner and movie night. Those stopped happening completely. Things like bowling, ice skating, or any type of "date night" became too strenuous now and all activity outside of our house stopped. Until February, I had at least been able to push myself on through and continue doing activities, even when they required more physical stamina, but when February came around, my life became so very different. Instead of making plans for a Friday night out with our friends, we had to sit at home. In fact, we rarely left the house. On few occasions friends would come to our house but I could not go to other homes because I was attached every second to the oxygen and bi-pap machines.

Obviously, a marriage has a physical side but when you can't breathe, can't walk across the room without heaving, or can't take a shower without the possibility of passing out, you are not well enough and physically fit enough for that physical side. Sometimes, it's just not possible no matter how badly you want to make it happen. I'm adding this part because it's important for you to know how I felt. I didn't feel like a human. I definitely didn't feel like a man or husband. I felt like I was losing what it meant to be "me." I felt like I had been stripped of some of life's most basic fundamental characteristics. I was frail, losing weight, coughing constantly, unable to do or be what I wanted to do and be, and on top of all of that, I couldn't be the husband I wanted to be for Sallie.

Our 8 year anniversary was in April of 2012 and we had to cancel our plans because I was too sick to really do anything. We did go and have a dinner but it was extremely difficult and we ended up back home very quickly. I simply couldn't breathe without the bi-pap continually on my face. This was a very hard time because I so desperately wanted Sallie to have everything and I so badly wanted to make it a great anniversary. We had seen for the past three months my steady decline and new our vacation wouldn't happen but we wanted to believe so much that God would heal me. Honestly, I was dying and we were praying but I kept getting worse. It was tough on our faith as a couple. Whether coughing uncontrollably in a spasm or whatever else, it seemed that no matter what happened, God was silent on the issue.

On May 2nd I woke up around 1AM with a bad coughing spasm but quickly realized that there was blood in my bi-pap face mask. I took it off and continued to cough blood into a bowl for a short amount of time. Of course, this wasn't the first time I had coughed blood but it was definitely the first time since being on the bi-pap. We called the doctor and were instructed to see him the next morning.

My PFT on that visit was 22%. My lower airway was 7%. I hurt everywhere and felt awful. My lungs were not working and of course I went into the hospital for another IV session. We had packed everything already and so I went directly to the hospital floor where they began the same therapies and meds as I've done for nearly 17 years now.

After 3 months of literally sitting in the house and not getting better, after 3 months of praying daily for a miracle, and after 3 months of missing out on life, I was drained. I hadn't been able to enjoy any time with Sallie. It is so important to me to be able to have fun and do awesome activities with Sallie and not being able to just about finished me off. I really felt that my life was over unless God healed me. Knowing that CF doesn't just reverse on its own, I really didn't have a very good outlook. Unless God healed me, I was not going to make it much longer.

I normally try to be cheerful and positive but this time I just didn't really feel it. I was quiet and didn't talk much. I remember thinking how strange it was that I didn't feel like talking at all to anyone. I am the guy that can talk to anyone in the world. I'm that guy that could probably hold a conversation with a wall if I had to but I didn't feel it this time. I was polite and friendly but just not my usual gung-ho self. So, I let others do the talking for once.

You can learn a lot about people when you choose not to talk. You find out that their concerns and problems are usually brought on by bad choices or by bad reactions to other things in their lives. You also find out how relative things really are to people. Most people just have no clue that they are so blessed in so many ways. My favorite thing to do was to listen to someone complain and moan about their difficulties while I was in the hospital, unable to even contemplate doing the very activity that they complained about. I don't know how many times I had to just shake my head at the constant whining that seemed to emanate out of the mouths of so many incredibly healthy individuals. I realized during that time just how much I really had to be thankful for and how blessed I really was to be able to be content even in a time that was extremely horrible. In fact, after listening to so many people having such horrible lives, I truthfully was able to see my life in a great and glorious way. Thank you to those people for helping me realize that even in the worst time of my life, I still had it better than them.

I had a few visitors during the next two weeks from work and church. I wasn't progressing but I also wasn't getting worse so that was good. I was alert and talking when I felt like it and overall it seemed just like any other normal hospital session. Sallie had even gone on her work trip to Houston since it seemed I was doing fine. I assured her I was feeling alright and that I'd be fine while she was in Houston. She left on Tuesday, May 14th. I was fine.

Sallie returned on Friday, May 18th to a husband that was in respiratory failure and dying.

The next week is foggy for me. I actually don't remember very much about the entire event but I do know that my lungs were failing, my carbon dioxide levels rose to critical levels, and I was going to die without a lung transplant. At some point I received a blood transfusion, was placed on a ventilator, and was placed on the emergency transplant list. Sallie has written a part of this chapter that will obviously hold much more detail about the events because I don't remember anything.

On Sunday, May 20th, my doctor, Dr. Santiago Reyes, informed my wife that I had only three or four days left at the most. I was in need of a double lung transplant immediately. With CF, when a lung transplant takes place, they have to have both lungs from a single donor to put into the patient. This means that for me to live, someone would have to die. Not only that, but they would have to be donors, their family would have to allow them to donate, and they would also have to be undamaged.

For most transplant patients, they are on a list for a long time. Many people are on lists for years due to blood types or organ availabilities and many people die because they are not able to get organs that they need. Also, many times the family will overrule the donor specification on the license and not allow the harvesting of organs, even though the person may have wanted to donate. This makes it extra difficult considering organs aren't something you can just go to the store and buy. If someone wants to be a donor, it doesn't always mean they will be. It's just the way it works. If you need lungs but no one passes away that is a donor, then you don't make it. If you need lungs but the family or person-in- power decides to not allow donation, then you don't make it. This was the situation I was in and statistically, it was a very bad situation.

On Monday, May 21st, I began to get a lot better. In fact, I was up and joking around with Michael Ray, one of my closest friends, and Melissa Mullins, my cousin. We were laughing and cutting up like teenagers again and I felt wonderful. I even was able to take my bi-pap off and breathe well. Even though on the surface this looked awesome, there was something much more serious taking place that very few people even know about. I was in the "surge."

The "surge" is a time period right before death when the body becomes extremely excited and begins to mimic healthy symptoms which are absolutely opposite of the way the body has been reacting. In my case, I began breathing well, laughing and joking, and even able to sit up and eat. Again, on the surface, most people would view this as improvement, but the nurses and doctors knew the truth. They knew that this was the very last thing before death.

It was the beginning of the end. I needed a set of lungs immediately or I would not make it.

Statistically, that just doesn't happen.

Chapter 14.2
These Lungs Will Praise The Lord

The Power Of 38

The weekend of May 18th – 21st marked the beginning of the end. Without a transplant I would not make it and the probability of a double lung donor with the correct needs was so small. Of course, people were praying everywhere and posts were on Facebook and Twitter constantly so a lot of people knew about my situation even though I did not. I believe without a doubt that the thousands of people praying worked and God answered, shattering statistics and probabilities as He usually does.

On May 21st a donor was found! Against all odds, a donor for a double lung transplant came through the hospital. Against every firm statistic, and with only about 12 hours left for my life, a donor for a double lung transplant was available. Three days ago, my doctor pronounced a death sentence and now, three days later, a donor is available, despite the odds that it wouldn't happen. Despite the understanding and knowledge that this kind of thing never takes place. Despite the medical intelligence and transplant experiences that reveal that 3-5 days isn't enough time to find organs for donation...

But God...

The donor was young and considered high risk. They had overdosed on heroin and had been brought into the hospital emergency center but had not lived. The young person had signed the donor check box on their license and the family agreed to let the harvesting of organs proceed. So, a viable set of lungs was available but with certain risk.

What if they had a disease from using drugs or from a lifestyle that usually accompanies addiction? This presented a very difficult scenario for us in that if I accepted lungs from a person that had a sexually transmitted disease or an illness acquired by using dirty needles, I could pass that to my wife. Of course, the diseases themselves would wind up making my life possibly worse.

I'm told I declined the lungs actually at first but I don't remember. My wife promptly told me what was up and I guess I listened to her because we accepted the lungs and they immediately scheduled me for surgery. After acceptance and getting scheduled, I'm told they barely got me into surgery in time. I don't remember a single bit though and that is why my wife has written her part of this story.

The night of the surgery was a horrendous night for everyone except me. I do not remember a single event or detail, which I will talk about later on. In the waiting room that night was a few groups of people. One small group with about 3 people, one single person, and another small group of 5 were all waiting in similar circumstances like my group was except for one difference. There were 38 people in my group. No kidding. 38 people came up to the hospital and waited in the surgery waiting area!

Moms, Dads, aunts, uncles, and cousins and lions and tigers and bears...they were all there! It was a crowded surgery waiting area filled up with family and friends from both sides of our family. Not only family, but friends also from work and church showed up. Coworker friends, youth pastor friends, missionary friends, pastor friends, and just about any other type of friend were there in that waiting area. I am sure it was strange to have a few small groups and then this massive clot of people overtaking the waiting area. They were all there and I'm sure they were all stressed and trying to figure out how to handle the situation.

So, my family and friends did the only thing they knew to do. They set up a prayer chain throughout the night with someone praying in 30 minute segments. Basically, people began praying without ceasing, organizing a way to keep prayer going for me continually. They gathered in the hospital chapel and prayed alone, together, and in groups. Some people prayed silently, some people prayed loudly, and others just kept their mind on the need for God to do the miraculous.

My pastor, Pastor Charles Clanton, preaches a message based out of scripture from Luke 12 where James is put to death by King Herod. When put to death, Herod sees that it pleases the Jews so he makes plans to also kill Peter. He orders Peter to be put into prison with every intention of killing him but the scripture sort of takes a detour for about half of a verse and makes mention of something very interesting that almost doesn't fit in the story.

Luke 12:5 – So Peter was kept in prison, but the church was earnestly praying to God for him. (NIV)

Pastor Clanton goes on to mention that there is no record of the church praying for James. But, when they pray for Peter, Peter is set free from prison by an angel of the Lord. His message goes on to ask the very pertinent question of what would have happened to James had the church prayed for him like they prayed for Peter?

I believe that I am alive because of the prayers of those 38 people. Those 38 people are the church that offered up earnest prayers to God for me. Those 38 people were from all walks of life, all levels of income, all races, and all denominations of Christianity. Some were beginners in Christ and others were elders and spiritual leaders in their local assemblies. Those 38 people did not all know each other, did not all believe the same things but were able to put aside differences to unite with one common goal. They were able to pray together, communicate together, and even fellowship to some extent together even though they all were so different that in normal settings, they probably wouldn't fellowship as readily.

There were Methodist, Baptist, Catholic, Pentecostal, and non-denominational believers and some non-believers joined with the unified mind to reach God. Pastors, youth pastors, music leaders, Sunday school teachers, and every other kind of leader in multiple churches all got together and reached for God, offering earnest prayer for me.

I cannot forget the thousands who were reached out to through social networking and texting. Those 38 contacted their churches and leaders who in turn contacted more people. In a conservative estimate, I believe nearly ten thousand were probably praying or at least had my situation on their minds. It spanned across the country and even into other countries through contacts and missionary groups. That's amazing to know that because of those 38 unified believers, thousands began praying and concentrating on my need and all the time I never knew.

I do not doubt at all that prayer and meditation on God is what not only caused the donor lungs to become available but kept me alive through the procedure. I lost lots of blood and the surgeon even said it was a rough surgery that had its scary moments but the church was earnestly praying to God for me. I know I am alive because of prayer. I know I am breathing and writing right now because of the 38 people and the thousands of others worldwide who were able to put aside differences and unify together in prayer for a common need.

I am forever thankful for the love, prayer, and power of those 38 believers. I realize that they are not the only ones who prayed but they represent everything I think of when I read the phrase "The Power Of 38." Thank you for supporting me and especially being there for Sallie.

Chapter 14.3
These Lungs Will Praise The Lord

A Peaceful Sleep

○ ○ ○ ○ ☐

Again, I don't remember much of what took place during the days before and after the actual surgery event. Crazy stories are told to me that I just have no memory of. I am told that I was lucid and in my right mind when signing the DNR and also signing the papers for the surgery itself. But I don't remember a single bit of it.

I am told that I was having conversations with people and acting completely normal leading up to the surgery, but I don't remember a single bit of it. I am told I even was talking immediately before the surgery to my Dad but I don't remember any of it.

Sallie convinced me to accept the lungs, but I don't remember any of it. I don't remember meeting the surgeon, signing papers, or anything. It's as if it didn't really happen. Except that I know it happened so I am left a little disconnected. In fact, it's this disconnection that has consistently bothered me. In a previous chapter, I mentioned I had "lost" some days while sick a few times but this is much more than days. I don't remember nearly two whole weeks.

I don't remember getting so sick that they called Sallie to tell her to come home. I don't remember having to choose a high risk lung donation and having to weigh the consequences that might have shown up. I don't remember feeling pain or illness at all. All I have during that time is a feeling of being asleep as it passed me by.

And that is what freaks me out. I could have died during those few days while waiting on the transplant donor and I would never have even known it. It's not like I saw death coming. For me, I just fell asleep one day and then woke up the next.

But when I woke up, I had undergone a double lung transplant that miraculously took place just in time. Had a donor not magically appeared just in time, and had the donor parents not allowed the donation just in time, and had the surgeons not gotten me into the surgery room just in time, and had they not gotten me on the bypass machine just in time, I would have died. It's very real to me how close I got to really dying and the strange thing that lingers is the fact that I wouldn't have known.

I simply would have gone to sleep and then woke up in eternity.

It's like a continuous flow to me. It's like life and death are not individual events but one continuous event that has no definite end. I wonder now that when people do die, do they know they are dying, or do they just wake up somewhere else as if they were asleep all along?

Sometimes it keeps me up at night. I think of the "what if" of dying and how I would have just been unaware. I realize yet again how out of control I really am when it comes to things that I think are controllable. Death for so many seems a definitive event because when viewed from the outside, we see it in time. But for me, I could have died without knowing I was even close to begin with.

I really began to tell something was up when I had visitors. They would see me and literally be in shock and awe at me being alive, sitting up, and eating. For a while I let it slide that they were so fascinated but finally I got the whole picture and Sallie brought me up to speed on how close to dying I had come. Even the surgeons were in awe. And finding out the truth of the closeness of death helped me to really understand the feelings and thoughts I was having towards that "blank" section of my memory.

Dr. Canaly, one of the surgeons, would constantly say, "What a miracle." And for surgeons to say that is definitely a miracle. Or he would say, "We got to you just in time, got you on bypass just in time, got the lungs in just in time. What a miracle."

It is a strange feeling to know you almost died and didn't even know it. I've been asked if I had a "near death experience." I experienced the most peaceful, restful, and calm experience in that I was completely asleep and at peace during probably the most traumatic event of my life. And maybe that was my "near death experience" after all because nothing about my "memory" of that moment makes sense or is natural in any way.

Jesus speaks of death as sleep in a number of scriptures and my entire life I've often wondered about this. Mostly we view death as a distinct, hard, or strict event that has definitive characteristics. We hear stories of people being drawn into a light at the end of a tunnel but I did not experience anything I've ever really heard, read, or seen in movies. What I experienced though has made me really think about death in a new way. It could be as if life and death are not separate, are not distinct or definitive, but different versions of what we consider being alive. One is of course alive on the earth and another is alive in eternity but there is almost a seamless, flowing transition. Not the jarring and shocking idea of death that we see portrayed in movies and books.

It's like you just wake up one day and you are no longer alive in body but alive in eternity without ever knowing or experiencing the pain and torture with which death is portrayed. And while this might make sense theoretically or theologically, it is not something that I can really explain well. I felt peace and an absolute absence of fear about the whole thing. True, I don't remember the pain or even the events of the surgery but when I woke up, I knew I was alive and still on Earth because that feeling of peace and comfort was gone. I'm logical and intelligent and I know you are thinking that it was just the anesthetic and drugs affecting me but I've thought about this nearly every single day. I've had drugs for years and there is a difference between a drug-induced euphoria and what I am talking about. Even now after 10 months it's a feeling that I can still completely recall and know that it is not natural. It's a feeling that is out-of-place in this world and I cannot seem to forget it.

In fact, when I actually woke up in the ICU room and the feeling of perfection was gone, I got really angry and sad all at the same time. I went from a perfect, calm, and peaceful rest to being awake again and I truly didn't expect to be alive because I had never felt anything like it. If there was a feeling that could characterize heaven, I was feeling it but when that feeling went away and I realized I was actually alive and still on this Earth, I just absolutely hated it. I opened my eyes, looked at the room, and immediately knew I was on Earth and no longer wherever I had been just moments before.

That was what it felt like. As if I was literally somewhere else and now I was back on Earth. I remember asking the ICU nurse where I was and he replied that I was in ICU. I remember what I said back to him which I'm sure he thought was insane.

"Well, that's just disappointing."

I no longer fear dying. I say that humbly because I am not wishing to die or even seem like I am some superman with no fear but I do not fear the process of dying because this experience has literally changed the way I view death. Like Job, I've heard all about the ideas of how we'll live in eternity and how we'll experience this awesome and amazing eternal life but now that I have had this experience, I feel like I know and have experienced something different and amazing which causes me to not fear the time when my physical life ends and the transition to my eternal life takes place. It won't be painful or traumatic but instead it will be peaceful, calm, and beautiful.

The transition from physical to eternal is probably a better way to phrase it even. Not death, but transformation, and one that is completely comfortable, peaceful, and even inviting.

One that you don't fear, but desire.

Chapter 14.4
These Lungs Will Praise The Lord

Recovery

○ ○ ○ ○ ☐

One of the first stories I was told was when I was first brought out of the surgery. Dr. Canaly, one of the surgeons, spoke with the family to update them on my status.

"The first thing I want to say is that we have had a miracle tonight" he began.

"We barely got him into surgery and honestly we weren't sure we'd even have a surgery because we weren't sure we'd get him started in time but a true miracle took place and it is all due to God."

Of course, my family was probably shocked to hear a surgeon say this.

During recovery after surgery, no one was allowed to visit me. For some reason, if anyone came in the room, I would literally freak out and start clawing at the bedside or clawing at my face. I would try in vain of course to raise myself up and reach out for the person. So, they restrained me so I wouldn't hurt myself.

I have coughed for 32 years so when I came out of surgery and began waking up, I began coughing. Not because I couldn't breathe but because my body had been used to breathing badly for so long that my baseline response to life itself was to cough. The nurses in the ICU had to literally calm me down and tell me that I could breathe even though I was telling them I couldn't. That's how much I have coughed. Even after a transplant with brand new, perfectly functioning lungs, my body still thought it had to cough.

I remember when waking up and hearing that someone in the ICU was having trouble. I don't remember what their problem was but I overheard somehow while barely functioning that another patient was in a lot of pain. For whatever reason, this touched me so much that I asked for the people around me to hold hands and help me pray for that patient to feel better. So here we are, praying for that hurting patient, and I've just been through a double lung transplant that nearly killed me and I am hurting so much that I am delirious.

I had this dream that I shared with Sallie and a few other visitors but I do not remember any of it. Me and a ferret, appropriately named Captain Ferret, were trying to take over Six Flags. A notorious ferret family was already running Six Flags so they had to fight this ferret family, but Captain Ferret's family did not trust me as much as Captain Ferret did, but I was more than sure that we would conquer the day and that Six Flags would soon be ours.

In another dream, my mom and Sallie were spies. They were bad spies when Sallie asked me why they were bad spies, I replied,

"Because you are Russian, duh!"

So there you go. Sallie and my Mom were bad Russian spies and I was an American spy that had been captured and was in the Russian chair, which was actually the recliner in the room that I was sleeping in, but in the dream the Russian chair was the interrogation torture chair. Weird stuff.

My uncle John Sacker is so awesome! I love him so much and he really was a big help during the transplant time. Being an anesthetist himself, he knew a lot about the surgical atmosphere and actually helped in some of the rather sticky situations when the other staff members didn't know exactly what to do. However, he really struggles with aiding people when they need a drink of water.

I woke up and asked for a drink of water. Nothing weird, nothing strange. Pretty normal if you ask me. My lips were really dry and I was really thirsty. So, John, wanting to be helpful, gets me a cup of water and carries it to my lips. I begin to move forward to sip it and somehow it ends up literally spilling out all over my hospital gown. And it's super cold! No harm right? I just ask for some more.

He brings it over to my mouth again and promptly spills it all over me again. I don't know if I laughed of not but that is truly funny to me now. I don't know how many more times he spilled the water on me but I don't remember it very well so it really doesn't matter even if I never got that drink of water.

The very first thing I remember after surgery is someone sitting very close to my ear and singing a song I've known since before I can really remember anything. Someone was sitting with me, rubbing my arm I think and singing "In The Name Of Jesus." It's an older song that goes as follows:

> In the name of Jesus, In the name of Jesus
> We have the victory...
> In the name of Jesus, In the name of Jesus
> Demons will have to flee...
> Tell me who can stand before us,
> When we call on his great name
> Jesus, Jesus, Jesus, Jesus,
> We have the victory

- Public Domain

I couldn't figure out who was singing it at first but after a few words I knew that it had to be someone that knew me pretty well to be singing a hymnal song. It was amazing to have someone singing that song of victory in my ear and it really was the perfect song to sort of wake up to. It was even greater to know it was Sallie.

Recovery was rough and I was so thirsty all the time and it seemed like I couldn't ever get anyone to pay attention to me. I remember trying to look out into the room to see if there was anyone around and I could barely see anything. It seemed like I was in a fog and I felt like I had those weird glasses people wear that makes everything really squished and fat like in those mirrors at the fair. And it seemed no matter how hard I tried, I couldn't talk. I'm sure it was the pain meds now but during that moment it seemed very strange and even a little frightening. I can see how some people might think they were abducted by aliens considering my nurses and family had large eyes and longer than normal arms every time I looked at them. Surely it was the meds? Or was it?

Recovery time while in the hospital came in three phases. The first phase was what I refer to as the "Out Of Control Of My Body" phase. While in ICU, I was literally unable to do anything. No matter how hard I tried, it wasn't going to happen. Of course, I'd just had a double lung transplant but I was still very uncomfortable and in pain. They dosed me like crazy with morphine which helped a lot but there was still pain and since I was doped up, I really don't remember much. It's a good thing too. I don't mind forgetting painful periods of time.

I do remember waking up one evening a little more cognizant and alert. I don't remember exactly what came over me but all of a sudden I was filled with this enormous amount of love for my wife. I began thinking about all the crap she had just gone through and how through all the years before this she had been such an amazingly loving and faithful wife. I started bawling my eyes out which sort of startled and scared my ICU nurse because he immediately started trying to assess what my pain or problem was. I told him there was nothing wrong and that I just really needed to see my wife right then. So, the wifey gets escorted in and I'm sobbing and emotional like a teenager in love and I proceed to tell her how much I love her and how awesome she is. My wife is amazing and I'm sure I waxed eloquently but I think I immediately fell asleep after.

During this phase also in ICU I really don't remember most of the visitors. I remember flashes of faces and even some people talking but overall it is vague and blurry. I know some coworkers were there and I remember distinctly "seeing" Lynnette, my manager from work. I remember hearing my Dad's voice praying and also hearing Tom, my father-in-law, but honestly I couldn't place much bet that they were even real. Even the ICU nurses seemed unreal to me even though I remember holding conversations with them.

The one thing I remember well though no matter how groggy was the fact that I could breathe. Not only breathe, but breathe really well. I could take deep, long breaths of air and not cough or wheeze or even rattle. I wasn't requiring oxygen anymore either. For years I had been tethered to the oxygen tanks and then completely immobilized by the need for the bi-pap machine and now I was breathing on my own at nearly 100% oxygen saturation levels. On room air! What a miracle!

My memory really kicks in though a day or so before getting moved off of ICU and into the regular transplant floor room. This phase shall be called "No Privacy, No Pride." The reason is because on this floor, I was still unable to do anything for myself but I was more aware and awake. There is nothing like having someone else clean, bathe, and wipe you after using the restroom. You are really forced to learn that you have to call out for help and you might as well get over yourself and all the hang-ups you might have with someone seeing you naked. You learn quickly that just using the bathroom takes more than two people sometimes and that is a humbling and very sobering experience. I am not used to using the bathroom and then calling out for aide due to an unforeseen problem. Basically, you just get over it, swallow that pride, and hit that call button because otherwise, you're just sitting in a pile of crap!

As a side note, all the nurses on that floor deserve serious respect and admiration because it takes a seriously devoted professional to clean up and take care of the things they do. You are awesome!

I had chest tubes coming out of both sides of my body that drained fluid from the lungs. These things are cumbersome at best and very painful if you jar them against the bed or if someone runs into them. Luckily, that didn't happen too much. But, I was forced to sleep on my back the entire time they were in. It was absolutely awful I have to admit. I am a side sleeper and having to sleep on my back was the single most uncomfortable position in the world. Of course, in the past when I couldn't breathe, lying flat on my back wasn't possible so even though I was uncomfortable, I still marveled at the ability to breathe.

It was during this time that I actually injured my back pretty seriously. Since I couldn't move myself, I would have to ask the nurses and staff to reposition me in the bed if I had scooted too far down. One night I guess I woke up and without thinking tried to lift myself up in the bed to scoot up and when I did I felt a searing pain shoot through the right side of my back nearly the entire length. It hurt really bad and continued to hurt for nearly two and a half months. No kidding, even after going home I was still hurting in my back from that pulled muscle.

I also lost a lot of feeling on my chest near the incision line, the right side of my back, and my left thigh where the bypass was positioned during surgery. I had a huge hematoma due to being on the bypass longer than anticipated from complications and oxygen issues. And I was swollen to where my feet and legs looked like elephant legs. At one point I actually got afraid my feet would explode and because I wanted to know, I actually asked the nurse. They sort of laughed and said no that I would not explode. Hey, I didn't know that and by the looks of things,

I was going to explode like a sausage that was too stuffed. Either way, I didn't like it.

I haven't regained much feeling in my chest area. One night while I was stretching and had my eyes closed my wife thought it would be funny to pinch my nipple. Of course, since I had my eyes closed she thought it would be this hilarious prank but I never even flinched. So, she pinched again. Still nothing. When I opened my eyes, she's staring at me with this confounded look on her face.

"What?" I ask because she's staring so weirdly at me.

"You didn't even flinch." She says.

"What do you mean?" I reply because I'm completely lost.

"I pinched your nipple and you didn't even make a sound or move. What's wrong with you?" she says. And of course, she's right because nearly everyone on the planet freaks if you twist their nipple and for me to just stand there as if nothing happened was really weird.

I start laughing and proceed to tell her that I can't feel anything in that area. Of course, she doesn't believe me so I let her twist my nipple again for good measure.

Yep, nothin'. Not even a little bit of nothin'.

My back has gotten much better though but I have random numb places that tend to itch. The problem is that I can't find the place that itches to actually scratch. It's very weird. Sometimes I can end up scratching a patch of skin that is far off from the actual itchy spot and it works. That's weirder.

The days in the ICU weren't as tough as the days in the recovery room there on floor 8 at Baptist hospital in Oklahoma City. Mainly because I don't remember the ICU stay very much at all. Daily I would have to confront the ever present lack of privacy and it really was an issue for me. I also had to daily confront the lack of control in motor functions such as just simply raising a fork to eat. At first, due to swelling of the hands and also due to the disabling effects of the pain medicine, I really couldn't feed myself. I ended up with more food on me and my chest than actually in my mouth. Using the bathroom was a super effort because instead of a nice bathroom, I had a small portable toilet that rolled to the bedside. Since I couldn't get myself out of bed, I had to have someone help me get up and get undressed. Like I said, even though I realize it was necessary and in fact the job of the nurses, it was still a very humbling experience.

Men like to be men and I am the same way. I don't want someone to have to baby me, clean me, and for sure wipe me. I know many people who are in their end-years have to endure this lifestyle but I am only 32 years old and it was embarrassing. I constantly found myself apologizing to the staff for having to do so many things for me that were fairly gross or usually private.

I remember one night trying to have dinner while having a room full of visitors. I really didn't want to dump food on myself but I was also really hungry so I proceeded to try to eat. I would slowly raise the fork to my mouth and about half the time the food would make it in and about the other half I'd drop most of it back on the plate. My hands were shaking badly and my back was hurting so bad that it made it nearly impossible to sit up and eat for any length of time. And, to top it off, everyone is quietly watching me eat. As I kept trying, I kept getting more and more frustrated. Finally, Sallie ran everyone out of the room to give me privacy to spill food all over myself. I felt like an elderly man who can't seem to make their bodies do the right thing. I sympathize completely with anyone that has lost functionality no matter what their age because it is absolutely awful. I lost count of how many times I got so frustrated that I would just cry.

It was during this phase that I learned about the high risk donor lungs that were currently in my body. It's weird to talk about lungs that were originally not yours that you are now using. The nurses came in from the transplant team and proceeded to help us with our medicine check list which contains around 40 pills per day. Anti-rejection meds and other fun stuff to keep my body from rejecting the lungs. And how the donor was high risk and could have had HIV, hepatitis, or any other terrible disease since they were a recreational heroin addict. When I heard that, I freaked out. Really, I did but not in the physical sense but more like a nuclear bomb exploded in my brain. I immediately got so worried and concerned for Sallie and how I might transmit a disease to her. I didn't hear anything else that the nurse said because my mind couldn't get around the concept of a high risk donor giving me some terrible disease that I could pass on to Sallie. The moment the nurse left the room, I couldn't hold it in any longer and just started crying. Sallie of course was shocked because I had been sitting there so still and kind of out of it. I felt like I had been through so much already and now this was just too much. I felt that I was a threat to Sallie's health by her being with me and that meant everything in our lives would have to change and would be even harder. I finally found out later that they had tested me and were continuing to test me for different diseases and that everyone always came back negative and I did not have any diseases.

I received lungs from a heroin addict after being given 3 days to live and did not get any diseases. Do I really have to explain how that came about after this much writing? It's so fun to say it though...

... But God ...

One night I was really hurting and none of the meds were helping. It was 3am and I was wide awake and my chest hurt like crazy. I was sitting in the dark feeling pretty bad about everything in general when one of the respiratory therapists comes in. Without saying anything, she walks over to me and lays her gloved hand on my forehead and begins praying. Her sincerity in prayer caught me off guard. I could feel her concentration and focus and it really touched me. She began to also speak in tongues which for me was a definite shock. Of course, I asked her about her faith and we talked for a while on many different topics but the one thing she consistently kept saying was to trust in Jesus because He had the power to take care of it and died to save us already. She talked about living for Him and giving our lives to Him and how much He really was involved even though we can't always understand His ways. After she left, I was struck with the realization that God had sent her to encourage me in a moment of pain and suffering. Yet again, God was doing the miraculous, reminding me again that He is always aware of us and intimately involved in everything that takes place in our lives.

Recovery sucks but I got through it. In fact, I excelled at recovery. I began rehabilitation for walking and exercise around the 2nd week. Rehab sucks but I worked hard. I remember the first time I actually walked after my transplant. The therapist came in and started working with me on how to stand up and then sit down which took an excruciatingly large amount of effort. I felt like my body weighed a ton and my muscles were completely useless. I had been in bed for nearly 2 weeks without moving and had lost most of my muscle mass. Trying to use those weak and dilapidated muscles again was a very frustrating and painful experience. After a few sessions of standing and sitting, we started the process of trying to walk.

They tied me to the therapist for support in case I began to fall and then we began. I had chest tubes coming out of my sides, an IV pole with meds running, and about four nurses to help me drag all of that along. I walked and they pulled the machines and meds down the hallway there on the floor. It was super slow going and I actually used a wheelchair to help me walk so I wouldn't have to hold myself up. I walked to the nurse station and back to the room extremely slowly but I made it. My body literally felt like a ton of weight. I will never forget that feeling of walking for the first time down that hallway with my huge swollen legs and my super heavy body. It was so awesome to finally be out of that room for the first time and get to see something else. It was also awesome that I didn't require an oxygen tank.

After that, I began gaining strength and walking more and more. I was still swollen like an elephant but the walking felt so wonderful after so much time in the bed. In fact, I quit sleeping in the bed because it was so much easier to get out of the recliners in case I needed to use the restroom. Also, being able to walk meant I could go to the bathroom and sit on a real toilet!

Hallelujah for a real toilet!

The chest tubes were a problem. They were sticking out of my sides like some cyborg hookup in a sci-fi movie and they were always in the way. I knew that if I could just endure until those things were pulled out, I'd be home free. And, finally, the time came to remove them.

I'd been in the hospital for nearly 5 weeks, 2 of which were in recovery, and the time came to remove the tubes. The surgeon came in early one morning and checked the tubes and insertion areas to make sure they were healthy. I was barely awake and he was really quietly speaking.

"You don't have to get up. Just turn a little to the side so I can remove this chest tube." He starts in while I'm barely conscious. So, being used to being told what to do, I just turn over a bit. It's not comfortable but worth it since I know he's removing the tubes.

"Now, when I count to three, I want you to take a deep breath and blow out all the way. This is going to pinch a lot." He tells me.

Now, I don't know if you remember the chapter that talks about how badly surgeons lie but if you do, then it is important for me to reiterate that yet again. Surgeons are notorious liars.

He said: *This is going to pinch a lot.*

Translation: This is going to hurt so much that you will nearly pass out and most likely will wish you had passed out.

He counts to three and I breathe in and then blow out all of my air and he pulls the tube out.

If I hadn't known better, I'd have thought that what he actually did was jam a knife directly into the hole in the side of my chest. Dear Lord, I literally saw stars and the entire room started spinning which until that moment I thought only existed in the cartoons. I think I even heard the tweety birds.

"Son of a motherless goat!" I exclaim because really, that's the only logical phrase that anyone could have yelled at that moment. Really, it was like he had taken a searing hot poker and touched my lungs. All down the left side of my body I felt fire and searing pain that basically sapped me of any energy I had actually gained from sleeping the night before.

"Breathe in and out slowly," he says in calm, soothing tones, "and try not to breathe too fast."

Easy for you to say Satan, because you're not the one who just had his lungs ripped out. After about 5 minutes the intensity of the pain began to subside and I was left with just a very unpleasant, dull pain.

The next morning, we repeated the same process all over again for the other side. Except this time, I thought I was ready and could handle it.

Nope.

"Son of a motherless goat!"

After that things were a breeze. And I mean that honestly. Those evil tubes were gone and I was free to actually walk around without being tethered to anything. It was like being set free from prison! I began walking laps on the hospital floor every day and my strength, stamina, and motor functions were returning to normal.

My last stay in the hospital is a time I call "Stupid" because I was sent to Jim Thorpe rehabilitation center for a week. I had already begun walking many laps per day and was able to dress myself, bathe myself, and use the restroom. But, I endured the last week, gained more strength through different exercises and was released to go home on June 16th.

The day I was released one of the therapists stopped by to pray for me. She came in and made a kind of goofy gesture and asked if she could pray with me before I left. There's nothing like the power of prayer.

Chapter 14.5
These Lungs Will Praise The Lord

Now To Live

○ ○ ○ ○ ▢

When I got home, it was so weird. I had been gone for a total of nearly 8 weeks and even my cat was freaked and almost didn't remember me. When I walked in, I noticed my house looked very different. All of my carpet had been replaced by wood flooring. Our parents had gotten together and bought and installed wood floors so we didn't have to have carpet. The nurses and doctors had all spoken about how bad carpet was for respiratory health, so our parents went and changed it for us. Wood floors are so awesome! I will never have carpet again. Thank you so much for that gift that truly has made a tremendous difference for me.

Oh to sleep in my own bed and lounge around in my own house without any interruptions from the nurses! Seriously, if you need rest, don't go to the hospital because someone on staff will walk in every single time you are about to fall asleep to strap a blood pressure cuff on or take your temperature. As if it's any different than it was 30 minutes ago!

I've taken it slow of course considering the immensity of the surgery that I had but I'm definitely a walking miracle.

I can breathe.

I go to sleep and sleep all night without waking up with spasms of coughing. I feel refreshed in the morning, ready to meet the day. I can walk and exercise, even outside. I can pretty much do anything I would ever want to do. I am a new person entirely.

For years my wife and I have had to live a very sedentary life because I couldn't physically do many of the activities and events that most people take for granted. We had grown accustomed to coming home after work and doing nothing except resting for the next day. Now, I come home and make plans to do things in the evenings. Now, I take walks with Sallie outside and I am enjoying every single second. I can walk an entire mile without coughing even one time. In fact, I almost never cough. It's weird.

I have coughed for 31 years. Every day of my life and nearly every minute of the last 16 years I have coughed, heaved, wheezed, and rattled every time I breathe but now, I am completely silent. There are no pops and crackles when I breathe in. Instead, there is just silence and the sound of air flowing normally.

It's a miracle and it's something I'll never get used to. Every morning I wake up and breathe in and realize I am not coughing, not straining for air, and not tired. Every day I marvel at the ability to breathe when I walk across the street for lunch or go on a date with Sallie. Every night I think back through the day and remember not having to cough.

I'm finally gaining weight and filling out instead of looking thin and tired. I am healthy for the first time as an adult. I came home with a weight of around 122 pounds and I am currently 141 pounds. Now that's awesome. CF people usually don't gain weight easily and I have gained basically 20 pounds in about 4 months!

Sallie and I are acting like we've been given a new life completely. And it seems that is the way it is because I can do things I haven't been able to do in nearly 20 years. I can spend time with her without being tired always and losing energy immediately. We went to Orlando, FL, for vacation and I went to the Disney parks from 9am to 10pm and walked the entire time. The next morning, we got up and went to another park for the entire day and all without coughing or tiring out. I was able to do everything with comfort and ease that I have not had in years and with an enjoyment that I have not been able to have ever. Even flying was awesome because I didn't have to take 3 machines with me just to breathe and live. I actually had fewer travel bags than my wife for the first time ever!

After the Florida trip I traveled with a local youth group from Mustang, OK as a special guest speaker for their youth retreat that was held at Robber's Cave State Park in Wilburton, OK. I did everything the young people did even though they are around 15 years younger than me. We rode paddle boats, canoes, climbed and hiked our way through the Robber's Cave trails, and played volleyball. We stayed up extremely late around a camp fire singing goofy songs and eating roasted marshmallows. We were super active and it was one of the most amazing weekends for me because I was able to do all of that without coughing, wheezing, rattling, or losing all of my energy. I was able to do all of that without an oxygen tank or bi-pap machine. I was able to do pretty much anything I wanted and I loved every single second! Oh, and did I mention I had a double lung transplant only 4 months ago as of this writing?

On Sunday morning of that youth retreat I spoke to them about the miracle of my life. Imagine revealing to a young group of students that they had been walking, climbing, hiking, playing volleyball, and having a blast with a guy that could barely walk across the room 4 months earlier? Imagine how much of a testimony it is to see a person who barely made it out of the surgery room alive acting as active, energetic, and fun as the teenagers attending the youth retreat?

What an honor and privilege it really is to share this testimony with the future generations so that they can know that our God is as awesome and powerful in our day as He has ever been! Thank you Empowered Student Ministries from Mustang, OK for making that weekend such an awesome event. You guys rock!

I'm back to life, happiness, and all of the things that I could not do for so many years. My wife and I have a new and awesome future full of whatever we can think of because God has performed such an amazing and wonderful miracle in our lives.

What a miracle it is...

I saved this one for last. My first time back to church was truly incredible. I remember sitting in the audience and singing the worship songs along with the praise team. For years I had been unable to really sing and generally just quit singing altogether because it required so much energy but on that night, I sang the entire time without coughing or losing breath once. I was able to lift my voice and worship God with my new lungs and as I was singing I had a strange thought about the person whose lungs were now in me.

The person had died from drug addiction. Most likely they were very young, maybe still a minor. Hooked at such an early age, they were headed for a very destructive end and ultimately found that end on May 22nd. I don't know why that person was the way they were and why they struggled with drugs. I don't begin to comprehend a life that is so messed up at that young of an age but what I thought about instead was how the lungs of that person were now praising God. The lungs of a person who had died from a heroin overdose were now inside of another person who will try to bring praise to God in every aspect of his life. The lungs will be used for singing praises to God and preaching the truth about God to anyone who will listen. The lungs will be used for God.

After the service was over, while talking to my pastor's wife, Norma Clanton, I told her all about how I was able to sing the entire service without coughing. I ended the talk with the phrase with which I've named this entire chapter.

These Lungs Will Praise The Lord!

Final Chapter
Closing Remarks

○ ○ ○ ○ □

Yes, I still have Cystic Fibrosis, and sometimes I'm going to have troubles from that, but the miracle I'm living is so overwhelmingly magnificent that most of the time, I forget I even have CF. My life is so different now that I almost can't even compare. I have a future that I can actually plan for instead of just wish for. I have a life that I can live and enjoy instead of just endure. And I have an amazing wifey who makes me so entirely happy and has helped me through everything. I am so blessed.

And she is so smokin' hot!

What a miracle...

There are a million stories I could tell that would make this book way too long so I have chosen to focus on the positive, funnier, happier, and lighter side of a story that could be told very differently. Life can be a tough road and I hope you enjoyed this writing and possibly found some encouragement from it. It's just the wild and crazy stories of a 32 year old, happily married man living through a complex and often horrendous disease. A 32 year old man who loves his wifey and loves life, living, and being alive!

I am a 32 year old man who has seen a fair share of struggles, trials, and tribulations. Yet, I have come out still kicking and screaming with no desire to give up. I'm a 32 year old man who plays the organ, rides a motorcycle, plays video games, eats sushi, and enjoys spending every moment possible with his amazing and awesome wifey.

I'm a 32 year old man who just also happens to have Cystic Fibrosis who just also happens to have received a miraculous lung transplant and now has a life that is so completely different and awesome!

The "Make A Wish" Foundation tries to make wishes come true for children that have terminal illnesses and may not grow to adulthood. Most kids want to go to Disney World. When I was a child, they actually asked me what I would wish for and my answer was,

"To spend the night at Bro. Whalen's house and play chess." That was my answer. Bro. Whalen was my first pastor at church. Even at the earliest ages, church and the things of God were my way of life.

I can't divorce my life from Christ. It is part of me at the cellular level for I have been reborn not of this physical world but of the spiritual. I am a new creation existing in and completely supported by Jesus Christ. I could have asked for anything in the world and probably have gotten it but I asked to just spend time with my pastor. Even now in adulthood I could ask for many things but one of my main wishes would be that you would also know God like I do. I wish with every fiber of my being that you would know God, know the power of my God, and come to know the breadth, length, depth, and height of the love of God. There is no power like the love and care of my God.

There are lots of things to say at the end. I guess the most important though is that I am thankful you took the time to read this book. I hope you were entertained by some of it, encouraged by some of it, laughed at some of it, maybe even cried at some of it, and experienced emotions because of it, and maybe even felt inspired.

To me, that is the definition of living. Experiencing emotions and being alive with feeling and hopefully sharing life with others. I know there are hard times. I know there are times you want to give up. I know there are times when you will be depressed and hurt but don't let those times define your life. Let the good times outweigh the bad. Let the laughter, excitement, joy, and happiness of just being alive be the thing that defines you. Don't be afraid of life.

I pray you experience everything you desire to experience and not hold back from fear or intimidation. I pray you look at people and the entire world around you and realize the beauty of everything.

I pray you live life and enjoy your "Imperfect Perfection."

Imperfect Perfection
By Jonathan Sacker

Acknowledgments

To my wife Sallie – Thank you for always being so awesome. I love you so much and have no way to repay you for the love and devotion you have shown to me. I know that my life has been so blessed by you. Thanks for reading all my "revisions" and putting up with me constantly talking about this subject or that subject in an effort to finish this book. Thanks for your support in this writing. Thanks for your support in this life. You are a great wifey!

To my family – I love you so much and appreciate every single one of you. All of you have supported me, prayed for me, and done everything you can to make this life with Cystic Fibrosis easier. Your contributions are not taken for granted and everything you have done is so intimately valuable to both me and my wife.

Dr. Santiago Reyes (and staff) is by far the most amazing and wonderful doctor that I have ever known. His care and true devotion to the healing profession is unparalleled. I truly believe you save lives by fighting for me and every other Cystic Fibrosis patient in your unwavering efforts in CF research and care. I know that words are not enough to thank you for everything you do but it matters to me to say them anyway.

Dr. Mirza and the transplant team – I'm alive because of you and your tireless efforts to help me. I know God placed you in my life at the perfect time. To Mikel and Kimber, even now as I write, you are so wonderful and so awesome. Thank you for your constant help even when I am grumpy from blood pressure problems!

To the medical staff – Thank you for your compassionate care and unparalleled professionalism and intelligence. I can't really put into words how much of a relief it is to walk through the doors of yet another hospitalization up on the floor and see familiar faces that are not only professional and intelligent but also loving, caring, and friendly. You make the hospital stays so much better and you truly are all angels of blessings to the patients.

To my "secret editors" – I'm sure you got tired of re-reading all my edits but I am truly thankful you stood by and hung in there. I am appreciative of the time spent helping me make this writing what it has become. Thank you so much.

To the "church" – Your prayers have saved my life many times. Thank you for the many hours you spent interceding on my behalf and speaking to God for my needs, not just during the transplant period, but throughout my entire life. Never forget that God answers prayer and that I am the living proof that God hears us and answers us when we pray in faith.

To God – Thank you for being such a great God.

Imperfect Perfection
By Jonathan Sacker

© 2012 Jonathan Sacker

Contact the author at:
ThisIsMyImperfectPerfection@gmail.com

Made in the USA
Lexington, KY
07 October 2014